TRANS/
PORTRAITS

Jackson Wright Shultz

TRANS/
PORTRAITS

VOICES FROM TRANSGENDER COMMUNITIES

Dartmouth College Press / Hanover, New Hampshire

Dartmouth College Press

An imprint of University Press of New England

www.upne.com
Manufactured in the United States of America

Designed by Eric M. Brooks

Typeset in Quadraat and Fresco Sans by Passumpsic Publishing

For permission to reproduce any of the material in this
book, contact Permissions, University Press of New England,
One Court Street, Suite 250, Lebanon NH 03766;
or visit www.upne.com

Library of Congress Cataloging-in-Publication Data

Shultz, Jackson Wright.

Trans/portraits: voices from transgender communities /
Jackson Wright Shultz.

    pages cm

Includes bibliographical references and index.

ISBN 978-1-61168-823-8 (cloth: alk. paper)—

ISBN 978-1-61168-807-8 (pbk.: alk. paper)—

ISBN 978-1-61168-808-5 (ebook)

1. Transsexuals—Case studies. 2. Transgender people—
Case studies. 3. Transsexualism. 4. Transgenderism. I. Title.

HQ77.9.S55   2015

306.76'8—dc23   2015005587

5 4 3 2 1

FOR THOSE
WHOSE TRUTHS
HAVEN'T YET
BEEN TOLD

CONTENTS

ACKNOWLEDGMENTS

First and foremost, I would like to thank the mentors who made this project possible. Myrna Frommer, thank you for providing countless hours of editing, critique, and questions. Thank you Annelise Orleck for giving me your time and opinion when you were so busy with activism yourself. Jack Turco, thank you for your thoughtful edits, for everything you have done for me, and for everything you continue to do for your patients and for trans communities. Thank you, Marci Bowers, for your wonderful insight and for reminding me of the importance of context. I also want to thank Linda Heidenreich-Zuñiga, who taught me the value of learning and recording queer history. And, of course, many thanks go to the First Friday Freaks who kept me upright this year.

This work would not have been possible without the interviewees, who were so willing to share their personal thoughts and experiences, and who continue their daily activist pursuits. It is my sincerest hope that, as a writer and educator on trans topics, their collective activism will one day make my job obsolete. I would like to also acknowledge the Leslie Center for the Humanities at Dartmouth, which provided partial funding for this research, and who recognized the value of recording trans history.

Last, innumerable thanks go to Kristopher Shultz: the love of my life and my greatest editor.

NOTES ON STYLE

First, there is a glossary at the end of the book that might prove helpful to those who are not as familiar with the vernacular of trans communities. The definitions provided are basic and subject to contestation, as many of the terms do not have a readily agreed-upon definition.

Second, there are several spelling decisions that I have elected to make. "Transexual" has been spelled with one s rather than two. This spelling is a reclamation of a term originally used within medical communities. The removal of the second s pulls the term away from the medical and Latin connotation of "crossing" sex and returns it to the hands of trans folk who might not wish to medically or surgically transition but who still identify as transexual. I have elected to spell trans man and trans woman with a space between the modifier (trans) and the noun. I recognize that some feel that the lack of a space between these words affirms the inextricableness of their status as a trans person from the rest of their identity. The language and spelling of trans vernacular is constantly evolving. If this spelling choice upsets, it certainly serves as a reminder of just how politically charged the activism of identity, labeling, and spelling can be.

Third, I use trans and transgender as umbrella terms and do so in the broadest sense. For the purposes of this book, trans includes anyone who has transitioned socially, medically, or surgically; anyone who identifies or expresses their gender in a nonconforming or nonbinary manner; and anyone who does not fit into a masculine/male, feminine/female dichotomy. It covers all manner of genderqueer or gender-bending expressions. It covers pre-, post-, and nonoperative or hormonal transitions. It covers a vast spectrum of people who are not cisgender or cissexual. Please know that I think of the terms trans woman, trans man, and genderqueer neither as a limited trinary of trans-spectrum identities nor as hastily applied labels. Instead, I think of each of these terms broadly as descriptive of a set of experiences with a certain degree of commonality. My goal in using such an extensive definition was to discover both the commonalities and differences among nonbinary identities and to find the commonalities within those differences.

A BRIEF TIME LINE
OF TRANSGENDER HISTORY
IN THE UNITED STATES

This time line pertains only to the United States. There are many cultures throughout the world that recognize third-gender categories, or have long traditions of genital-reassignment practices. It should also be noted that many of the early surgical and medical advances in transgender health occurred in Europe. Recent advances in this field are primarily coming from Asia, South America, and the Middle East, with Thailand and Iran being the current world leaders in genital-reassignment surgeries.

Precolonization / Over 155 Native American tribes recognize third-gender categories. Third-gender assignments ranged from forced to chosen, revered to shunned.

1400–1600s / Colonialists enslave, kill, or forcibly convert indigenous peoples to Christianity, particularly those embodying nonbinary genders or sexualities.

1770s / Deborah Sampson and several other women disguised themselves as men and enlisted in the Continental Army during the American Revolutionary War.

1840s / Municipalities begin passing statutes that criminalize cross-dressing.

1861–1865 / At least 240 women disguised themselves as men and enlisted in the Union and Confederate armies, a number of whom continued to live as men after the Civil War concluded.

1918 / Ralph Werther publishes *Autobiography of an Androgyne*, a first-person account of belonging to a "third-sex" category.

1940s / Louise Lawrence starts extensive correspondence network with trans folk throughout the United States and Europe.

1949 / Physician Harry Benjamin begins to provide hormone replacement therapy to trans patients in the United States.

1950s / Elmer Belt becomes the first-known surgeon to begin performing genital-reassignment surgery in the United States.

1952 / Christine Jorgensen becomes a media sensation in the United States after receiving genital-reassignment surgery in Denmark.

1953 / *Jet* publishes article about Carlett Brown, billing her as the first "negro" to pursue genital-reassignment surgery. It is unknown whether Carlett was successful in accessing surgery.

1964 / Reed Erickson founds the Erickson Educational Foundation to fund research on transexualism.

1966 / Harry Benjamin publishes *The Transsexual Phenomenon*, arguing for compassionate clinical, medical, and surgical treatment options for transexual patients.

1966 / *Anonymous v. Weiner* court case petitions the New York City Department of Health to change the sex of the petitioner's birth certificate, after she had undergone genital-reassignment surgery. The court ruled that the sex on a birth certificate could only be changed if an error in recording was made at the time of birth.

1966 / Johns Hopkins University Gender Identity Clinic founded. Avon Wilson is the first client at the center and the first recorded African American to undergo genital-reassignment surgery.

1966 / Compton's Cafeteria Riot occurs in San Francisco to protest police harassment against trans folk, queer homeless youth, and sex-workers.

1967 / Conversion Our Goal (COG), the first-known trans peer-support group, is founded in San Francisco.

1969 / Riot occurs in response to police raids on the Stonewall Inn, a gay bar in New York. After Stonewall, many trans folk work to help develop the Gay Liberation Front but leave the organization when trans issues are omitted from the group's agenda.

1970 / Street Transvestite Action Revolutionaries (STAR) is founded by Sylvia Rivera and Marsha P. Johnson, to help queer street youth find food, clothing, and shelter.

1973 / Homosexuality removed from the *Diagnostic and Statistical Manual of Mental Disorders* (DSM). The next edition (DSM-III) included an entry for gender identity disorder, effectively pathologizing transexualism.

1976 / A New Jersey court rules postoperative trans folk can marry as their new sex designation.

1977 / Renee Richards becomes the first transgender person to play in the US Open after court rules that she is eligible to play in the women's division.

1977 / California becomes first state to allow trans folk to obtain a new birth certificate with the correct gender marker after undergoing genital-reassignment surgery.

1979 / Janice Raymond publishes the *Transsexual Empire*, a radical second-wave feminist critique of transexualism, justifying antitransexual prejudice.

1980 / The Harry Benjamin International Gender Dysphoria Association (HBIGDA) to promote standards of care for transexual patients is founded. Renamed World Professional Association for Transgender Health (WPATH) in 2006.

1986 / Louis Sullivan founds the organization that would later become FTM International, an organization dedicated to the advancement of the female-to-male (FTM) community.

1987 / AIDS Coalition to Unleash Power (ACT UP) formed in New York to respond to the AIDS pandemic and advocate for people living with AIDS.

1987 / Sandy Stone publishes "The Empire Strikes Back: A Posttranssexual Manifesto" in response to Raymond's *Transsexual Empire*.

1991 / Nancy Burkholder is removed from the Michigan Womyn's Music Festival for violating their womyn-born-womyn policy. In 1992 and 1993 protests are held within the festival.

1994 / Camp Trans is held near the entrance to the Michigan Womyn's Music Festival to protest gender policing and trans oppression in women's communities.

1995 / Riki Wilchins founds the Gender Public Advocacy Coalition (GenderPAC), an association of organizations that focused on addressing gender discrimination in workplaces and schools.

1997 / Gender Sphere forms. Based online, it was the first widely known national organization for genderqueer and gender nonconforming people.

1999 / First Transgender Day of Remembrance (TDOR) is observed to honor the life of Rita Hester, a trans woman of color who was murdered a year prior in Massachusetts.

2002 / First clinical trial conducted by the National Institute of Allergy and Infectious Diseases to study interactions between hormone replacement therapy and antiretroviral medications for the management of HIV.

2002 / Transgender Law Center founded to provide legal services and policy advocacy.

2003 / National Center for Transgender Equality founded to lobby for federal policy change.

2006 / Kim Coco Iwamoto is elected to Hawaii Board of Education, becoming the highest-elected trans official in the United States.

2009 / Trans Murder Monitoring Project is founded to collect data on trans homicides worldwide.

2010 / The State Department amends policy to grant gender-marker changes on passports without requiring genital-reassignment surgery.

2013 / The DSM-V revises the entry on gender identity disorder to gender dysphoria.

2014 / Susan Stryker and Paisley Currah publish *Transgender Studies*

Quarterly, the first nonmedical academic journal covering transgender issues.

2014 / California becomes the first state to ban the use of the trans panic defense in murder trials.

CHARACTER REFERENCE

ALEXANDER self-identifies as female-to-male (FTM), ace,
polyamorous, and pan-Asian.[1] He is a student at the University
of Florida studying public policy. He lives with his partner Huy
and their cat and dog.

ASH is the co-owner of a garden and farm supply store in Portland,
Oregon. She is interested in sustainability and urban gardening.
She identifies as nonbinary.

BELLA was an ensign in the US Navy as a young adult. She
disclosed her identity as a trans woman to her family when
she was fifty-two. She enjoys gardening and spending time
with her wife, children, and grandchildren.

BLAKE is a professor of disability studies at the University of
Colorado. He transitioned FTM while pursuing his PhD. During
the summers, Blake returns home to tutor and mentor youth on
the Fort Mojave Reservation.

CAMERON identifies as a transexual man. He came out shortly after
graduating from Mount Holyoke College. He recently left his
internship with the Trans Youth Equality Foundation to pursue
his interests in poetry and writing and spend time with his
fiancé, Grey.

CATHERINE is an orthopedic nurse at Princeton University Medical
Center. She transitioned male to female (MTF) while she was
a school nurse. She lives with her partner on their farm. She is
fifty-nine.

Some names and identifying information have been changed for issues of safety.
1. See glossary for explanations of identity terminology.

DAKOTA identifies as agender and uses ze/hir pronouns. Ze came
out to hir family when ze was twenty-six. Hir transition has
included surgeries without hormones. Ze currently works in
the college of nursing at the University of Vermont.

DIANE was a registered nurse until her multiple sclerosis
caused her to retire early. She volunteers with a social-justice
organization based in Washington, DC, that focuses on
bathroom accessibility. She lives with her partner who, like
Diane, also identifies as asexual and transgender.

ERIK is a butch-identified trans man. He transitioned as an
undergraduate student at the University of Idaho. He is
currently pursuing a PhD in women's studies at the University
of Washington and lives with his husband in Seattle.

FELIPE is a project-controls professional for a multinational
construction management company in Alaska. He spends
much of his time traveling and visiting his family.

GREG is studying accessible architecture at the University of
Pennsylvania. He also works as a volunteer each year at the
Philadelphia Trans Health Conference. When he graduates
he would like to move to the Netherlands to study public
transportation.

HILLARY works as an organic chemist and a pharmaceutical
researcher in Virginia. She transitioned MTF while she was
an undergraduate. She volunteers regularly for Planned
Parenthood and other local reproductive rights organizations.

HUGO grew up in a fishing family in Provincetown, Massachusetts.
He currently works in a fish market and drives a taxi in the
evenings. He lives with his partner, who is also trans.

JAIME identifies as genderqueer and uses the singular "they" as
their preferred pronoun. They work as a research assistant for
the University of Connecticut Health Center. They live with their
partner in Middletown.

JUANITA grew up in Wyoming but moved to San Francisco after
she dropped out of high school. She is currently between

jobs but hopes to find work cleaning houses. She is active in
ACT UP.

KELLY came out to her family as a girl when she was twelve. Her
family was very supportive of her transition, and she was able
to take puberty-suppressing medications and later hormones.
She is a student at the University of Northern Iowa.

KURTIS grew up in rural Oregon. He disclosed his transmasculine
identity to his mom when he was fifteen and started hormone
therapy when he was seventeen. He currently works for a
racial-justice organization and volunteers as a safer-sex
educator. He is twenty-five now.

LACY identifies as fae and prefers feminine pronouns. She provides
mental-health care to low-income individuals and families in
New York City.

LUIS transitioned FTM as an undergrad at Dartmouth College.
Upon graduating he moved to New York City to pursue a career
as an actor. He is currently working for the Callen-Lorde
Community Health Clinic in Chelsea.

MIRIAM is a student at Swarthmore College in Pennsylvania. She
transitioned as a senior in high school. She is studying adaptive
technology and is very involved in her campus Hillel (a Jewish
campus organization).

MOSLEY recently left her position as an assistant dean and the
advisor to black students at Dartmouth College. She identifies
as stud, boi, and masculine of center. She is a founder of the
online community Queer BOIS.

NATALIE is a police officer in rural Ohio. She transitioned on the
force when she was thirty-six and now provides lesbian, gay,
bisexual, and transgender (LGBT) sensitivity trainings to other
police officers. She lives with her wife and three children.

OLIVIA is a minister at a chapter of the United Church of Christ.
She transitioned when she was forty-three, after her two
children both came out to her as gay. She lives with her wife
in North Carolina.

OWEN grew up in Alabama but moved to Massachusetts to transition. He is now a mechanic in Boston and lives with his wife and their two children.

QUINN attended Wesleyan University as an undergraduate and majored in physical education. He currently lives in Portland, Maine, and lobbies for the decriminalization of marijuana.

RAFAEL identifies as stud and aggressive, and uses the pronoun yo. Yo works for a social-justice organization in Chicago that focuses on providing legal advocacy for transgender inmates and immigrant detainees.

RUSS identifies as transmasculine and uses the pronouns ze and hir. Ze attended Gallaudet University and now works for the Human Rights Campaign. Ze performs Deaf poetry in hir spare time.

SETH identifies as genderqueer and has a long history of involvement in queer and trans activism. He works as a crisis social worker in the San Francisco Bay Area.

SUPRIYA moved to the United States from India fifteen years ago to pursue her MD. She transitioned while she was a medical student at the University of Washington and now works as a doctor of internal medicine in New York.

TAYLOR is finishing her master's degree in anthropology at Washington State University, where she currently works as a teaching assistant. She transitioned when she was a sophomore in college.

VICKY lives with her parents in New Mexico. She would like to study cosmetology.

WENDY formerly worked as an investment broker for a large, multinational corporation. She and her teenaged stepdaughter transitioned MTF within a few months of each other. Wendy transitioned when she was in her sixties.

WILSON is a senior in high school. He enjoys acting but hopes to be a lawyer when he finishes school. He lives in Nebraska with his mother and brother.

ZACH lives in rural Vermont with his partner. He currently works as a photo developer for Kodak.

Although we cannot remember them, our first experiences in the world are typically based on our sex. Following the cry of "It's a girl!" or "It's a boy!" we will be given a pink or blue armband, respectively. From that moment we have been assigned a gender based on our biological sex. Girls will frequently be socialized to play with dolls, to spend time indoors, and to be passive. Boys will often be socialized to play with toy cars, to spend time outdoors, and to be assertive. We will spend the next years of our lives meeting or failing the gendered expectations that friends, family, and society have placed upon us. Most will conform to the gender they have been assigned. The following is an oral history of thirty-four individuals who did not.

All of these individuals fall into the broad category of transgender. As an umbrella term, trans or transgender describes anyone who feels discomfort with the gender they were assigned at birth. Some trans individuals physically transition, a process wherein a person takes medical steps to bring their body more in line with the gender with which they identify. Others forgo medical procedures and transition socially, taking nonmedical steps to express their genders in the ways that are most in line with the gender with which they identify.

Whether socially or medically, transitioning from one gender to another is always a complicated process. There are medical and legal difficulties that must be considered, and there are also social barriers that must be crossed. Although many people recognize their transgender feelings at an early age, they are not always presented with the information or resources needed to make an informed decision about transitioning. Increasingly, trans folk are disclosing their trans identities at younger and younger ages, but in older generations there still exist many trans folk who felt forced to suppress their feelings and desires for years in order to better assimilate to a dominant culture that encourages prescribed binary gender roles. There are those who transition neatly from one gender to the next, and there are others whose gender identities are fluid and frequently changing. Of the thirty-four individuals included in this book, none used the same terminology to refer to themselves.

One of the challenges I faced in writing this book was the inadequacy of the English language for discussing gender. For example, several of the interviewees preferred to use gender-neutral pronouns.[1] These pronouns look and sound unnatural, but that same awkwardness can make a pointed political statement about how ingrained a binary gender paradigm is in the dominant culture of the United States. Adequate terminology likewise failed many of the individuals I interviewed, and they often turned to slang (a form of expression that has unfortunately been delegitimized in many socioeconomic contexts). The breadth of words that trans communities have invented or reclaimed is astounding, political, and poignant. The terminology they use is often critical to conveying their gender identities and expressions, and creating and using these terms is frequently an important part of their daily activism.

The experiences of each of the interviewees differ greatly based on factors such as race, ethnicity, socioeconomic status, age, ability, sexuality, HIV status, religion, and a plethora of additional social influences. The characters are so diverse that I often felt they had very few common denominators. However, one of the commonalities I discovered was an overwhelming involvement in activist endeavors. Their definitions of activism were as varied as their gender expressions, but every single interviewee participated regularly in activist pursuits. From large protests to political lobbying and from educa-

---

1. Pronouns that do not convey a binary gender. See glossary.

tional outreach to using a set of pronouns that sparks a conversation—each of the characters told me stories of engaging in activism in their everyday lives.

This project has been an incredible journey. I have had an amazing opportunity to delve into the stories of dozens of incredible transgender individuals. The accounts they gave me of their lives were both inspiring and heartbreaking as we probed into the uncharted territories that lie beyond the gender binary.

A Historical Rationale

While transgender history certainly predates Christine Jorgensen, she was the first trans individual to receive widespread media attention in the United States when she returned from Denmark after having genital-reassignment surgery. A former GI during the Second World War, her stunning transformation caused not only a media explosion but also an upswing in transgender medical research and practice in the United States. She rose to prominence in trans communities along with her physician Harry Benjamin, who would establish international guidelines for providing health care to transgender patients. Much of the scientific and medical research about trans folk occurring at this time was quietly sponsored by Reed Erickson, a transgender millionaire philanthropist and patient of Benjamin's. This research helped to lay the foundation for medical transition, and the Erickson Educational Fund developed informational leaflets that provided information to trans folk on medical and legal matters relating to transition.

In 1966 Benjamin published the results of his work with trans patients in his book *The Transsexual Phenomenon*. Along with Benjamin, other endocrinologists, surgeons, physicians, and therapists, who utilized the clinical word "transsexual" to describe their patients, wrote the first wave of literature about transgender individuals. They created and shaped the medical precedents that still affect who can access trans-related health care and how.

Although transition-related health care increasingly became the subject of study, it wasn't readily available to trans folk in the United States throughout much of the twentieth century. However, the thought that transition was slowly becoming a possibility bolstered trans activists, cross-dressers, street queens, and drag performers to take collective action. Two important riots (the Compton Cafeteria Riot in San Francisco in 1966 and the Stonewall Riots in New York City in 1969) resulted as a backlash to police brutality against lesbian, gay, bisexual, and gender-transgressive individuals. Drag queens, streetwalkers, and other gender-transgressing frequenters of the respective establishments were influential in both riots, which marked a turning point in a movement that would be dubbed "gay liberation" and would come to reject the gender transgressors who had initially helped to surge the movement forward.

Among other goals, the gay liberation movement sought to declassify homosexuality as a mental illness in the *Diagnostic and Statistical Manual of Mental Disorders* (DSM), repeal legal bans on sodomy, and push for social acceptance of same-sex couples. Many trans folk felt that these goals ignored the issues that were most pressing to them and broke away to start their own movements, instead focusing on issues of unemployment, housing discrimination, and access to competent medical care. Gay liberation and trans liberation intersected in many ways, but when push came to shove, trans issues were often sidelined. In 1973 when activists did finally succeed in declassifying homosexuality as a mental disorder, a new diagnosis was added in its place: the next addition of the DSM included an entry for gender identity disorder, effectively pathologizing gender variance as a mental illness.

This pathologization of trans identities created a medical basis for a second wave of trans-focused literature, this time from an anti-trans perspective. These writings were penned primarily by second-wave radical feminists who believed (at best) that because trans women had been socialized as males they could not understand women's oppression, and (at worst) that trans women should be excluded from women's spaces and organizations because they were attempting to "infiltrate" women's organizations in order to subvert them through patriarchy. In 1979 Janice Raymond published her book *The Transsexual Empire*, which argued the latter point and was revered by trans-exclusionary radical feminists. Anti-trans politics such as these were put into practice most notably by the Michigan Womyn's Music Festival, which has long used the rhetoric that only womyn-born-womyn can attend the annual festival and has rejected trans women from the grounds of the festival on multiple occasions. In response, trans activists established an encampment outside of the festival grounds known as "Camp Trans" to support trans inclusion at the festival and to protest the exclusionary politics of the festival organizers.[2]

Several of the activists involved in Camp Trans are responsible, in part, for a third wave of trans-focused literature. Rooted in third-wave feminism and queer theory, this third wave has been primarily academic or historical in nature. Included are the historical works of Leslie Feinberg and Susan Stryker as well as a canon of queer-theory literature that includes works by Eve Kosofsky Sedgwick, Judith Butler, Judith Halberstam, José Esteban Muñoz, Julia Serano, Patrick Califia, and many others.

Within this third wave of literature, the research of sociologists and trans-advocacy organizations has made significant progress toward identifying issues prevalent within transgender populations. Because transgender is an umbrella term that encompasses a wide array of people, it has been difficult to obtain accurate and consistent data about trans populations. Some of the individuals who identify under the transgender umbrella will take steps herbally, medically, or surgically to transition, while others will only transition socially. Partially due to the broadness of this term, it is extraordinarily difficult to determine the prevalence of transgender individuals. Quantifying the prevalence of transgender individuals is also difficult

---

2. See chapter 6 for a personal account of this event.

because some who consider themselves fully transitioned no longer identify as transgender; many are suspicious of studies that ask them to identify as transgender; some studies undertaking this task were conducted in medical or mental-health settings, which are not always accessible to transgender patients and might only gather data on those who are seeking medical transition; and many do not feel comfortable disclosing gender-identity information for reasons of safety especially in studies that are not fully anonymous.[3]

While it is unknown exactly how many trans folk currently live in the United States, research has shown that trans folk experience high levels of discrimination and violence, as well as housing and employment instability, and often lack access to medical care and education. As of this writing, it is still possible to be fired in thirty-three states for being transgender, and a 2011 national survey on transgender discrimination found that 47 percent of respondents had been fired by their employer, denied a promotion, or not hired in a position because they were transgender.[4] This marked instability in employment often leads to lower socioeconomic statuses amongst trans folk. Additionally, the violence faced by trans folk is incredibly high. The National Coalition of Anti-Violence Programs found in their 2012 report on "Lesbian, Gay, Bisexual, Transgender, Queer and HIV-Affected Hate Violence" that LGBTQ individuals living with HIV, transgender individuals (especially trans women), and transgender people of color (especially trans women of color) are recipients of the most severe and often deadly forms of violence.[5]

---

3. Also, the word *identify* is often specific to certain racial and class contexts of gender. A study participant might meet the definition of transgender without "identifying" as transgender, or understanding what it means to identify due to the multiplicity of definitions of the word.

4. See Jaime M. Grant et al., "Injustice at Every Turn: A Report of the National Transgender Discrimination Survey, Executive Summary," National Center for Transgender Equality and National Gay and Lesbian Task Force, Washington, DC, 2011.

5. See National Coalition of Anti-Violence Programs, "Lesbian, Gay, Bisexual, Transgender, Queer and HIV-Affected Hate Violence in 2012," New York City Anti-Violence Project, 2013, p 32.

While the above research and literature has played an instrumental role in shaping how trans folk are perceived in and by academia, it has remained largely inaccessible to many trans individuals who lack access to formal educations. What little research is available raises a plethora of questions: Within transgender communities, why does gender-based violence and discrimination disproportionately impact trans women? How do factors such as race, ethnicity, religion, (dis)ability, socioeconomic status, educational attainment, and sexuality affect the experiences of trans folk? What role does geography play in these experiences?

The need for a fourth wave of trans literature written by transgender individuals that is simultaneously accessible to the majority of trans individuals is apparent. A number of authors have bravely begun this sojourn, but there is much left to be accomplished. The goal of the following project was to create a comprehensive, collective, and lay memoir of transgender experiences. Although this is a difficult undertaking, oral history seems the best medium to accomplish this task, as it allows trans individuals to tell their own stories in their own words.

The Vocabulary I Had Been Lacking

While many transgender people recognize cross-gender feelings at an early age, they are not always presented with the information or resources needed to make an informed decision about whether socially or physically transitioning might be right for them. Trans folk often suppress their feelings and desires for years because they lack the vocabulary needed to express their gender identity to others, because they wish to (or are forced to) better assimilate to a dominant culture that encourages prescribed binary gender roles, because they do not know that transitioning is an option, or because the most commonly discussed trajectories for transition do not fit with their own sense of self.

Some are not allowed to explore gender identities and expressions in their youth due to familial or cultural expectations surrounding gender. There are also sex disparities that influence who is allowed to bend gender rules. Individuals assigned female at birth (AFAB) are often allowed more flexibility to explore and embody a greater spectrum of gendered activities in their youth than are individuals assigned male at birth (AMAB).[1]

The first step in disclosing a trans or gender-nonconforming identity often involves deeply exploring the concept of gender and discovering that gender is not necessarily the strict binary we typically

---

1. Arguably, individuals assigned male at birth are not allowed to explore feminine gender roles due to societal devaluation of femininity and the feminine. See glossary for AFAB and AMAB.

believe it to be. Recognizing that transition is an option, developing vocabulary around trans issues, and accepting that some of this vocabulary might apply to them personally were among the initial obstacles facing many of the interviewees.

KURTIS

I was a tomboy when I was a kid. There is not a single picture of me before junior high where I don't have a short haircut. Whenever we'd go to the salon I'd look through the haircut books and I'd always reach for the boy's book. My mom would tell me I had to pick from the girl's book, so I'd pick the shortest haircut I could find.

It was okay to be a tomboy up until the time I hit junior high. Once you get to about twelve or thirteen, it's no longer socially acceptable for a girl to be so rough and tumble. I grew my hair out, and I tried to wear makeup and dresses, but I felt wretched about it. After months of attempting to assimilate to what the other girls in my grade were doing—and failing miserably—I tried to kill myself.

I took a cocktail of prescription and nonprescription medications. Luckily for me, prescription death isn't instantaneous. I had a lot of time between when I took the pills and when they started to work. I became terrified. I ran into my mom's bedroom in the middle of the night and told her what I had done. She drove me to the emergency room where they induced hours of vomiting to get everything out of my system.

My follow-up care required me to see a psychiatrist and to take antidepressants. The problem was, it didn't treat my depression. Depression was merely a symptom of a larger issue, not the problem itself.

It wasn't until I was fourteen that I finally figured out the cause for my depression. I was flipping through a *Teen People* magazine, and I found an article about transgender youth. I read the article over and over again. It's been ten years, and I still have that magazine stashed away in my closet. That article gave me the vocabulary I had been lacking my entire life. I finally knew what I needed to do.

BELLA

I transitioned when I was fifty-two. My whole life I had known I was different, but I could never put a finger on what exactly the problem was. As a poor, black man I felt that college was beyond my reach, so like most of my high school buddies I joined the navy.

The great thing about being in the military was that I didn't have to think. People told me what to wear, when to eat, when to sleep, [and] when to use the latrine. I liked being a sailor because all of my decisions were made for me, and I didn't have to think about who I wanted to be.

When I got out of the navy and had more time to think, I realized that I had all of these *feelings*. I didn't know what to do about them, but *oh, were they there!* I talked to people, and I did some reading, but the tales I heard over and over again were about white gay men who transitioned to become straight women. Well, there wasn't any place for a man who was attracted to women [and] who wanted to be a woman himself. I couldn't find myself reflected in their stories.

That's the problem. When you're a person of color, your stories just aren't told. Even now that I can look up whatever I fancy on the Internet, I can hear all of these stories and I can find all of this information, but none of it is my truth.

For years and years we've been put under the magnifying glass while white doctors and psychiatrists have written volumes of books about us, and we haven't got to say a word about it. Our voices have been silenced long enough. It's about damned time that somebody let us tell our truths.

QUINN

I grew up on Long Island and went to Wesleyan University for my bachelor's degree. Wesleyan has a pretty accepting campus and a seemingly disproportionate number of queer students,[2] so I was pretty familiar with trans issues and identities. I had multiple

2. Here, queer is used as an umbrella term for LGBTQI people. See glossary.

friends who were trans or genderqueer,[3] and I had complicated relationships with many of them. One of the trans guys I dated ended up making me feel very uncomfortable in our relationship, and I found out later that he had sexually assaulted a friend of mine. Another trans guy I knew slept with my girlfriend behind my back. All of my personal relationships with trans men were destructive,[4] and this colored my opinion of trans people negatively.

During my freshman year of college I started dressing more masculine. By my sophomore year, I was dressing almost exclusively in men's clothes and thinking about my masculinity a whole lot more. Even though I was questioning my gender identity a lot, I couldn't bring myself to identify as a trans man because I really hated the trans men in my life, whether justified or not.

I studied abroad in Nicaragua during the fall of my junior year. There really are no gender-variant people in everyday life in Managua, so I was a total anomaly. I got called "sir" all the time, despite the fact that I wasn't binding[5] and my hair was not incredibly short. I felt safer, and I wasn't getting harassed on the street like my female friends were. I quickly realized that wasn't the only thing that I liked about being mistaken as a man. There was a huge part of me that would become ridiculously elated every time someone called me "sir." I became incredibly comfortable with the masculine titles and pronouns that strangers were using for me.

I figured if I was totally comfortable interacting with people as a man in Nicaragua, it probably applied to the United States too. When I got home, I immediately tried out binding and realized I felt so much more comfortable when others thought of me as male. After several months of binding, and even shaving my head, I was still unwilling to switch pronouns. It wasn't until I graduated and

---

3. See glossary.

4. A trans man is often a person assigned female at birth who has taken social, medical, or surgical steps to physically or socially masculinize his gender expression or body. See glossary.

5. Flattening one's breasts. See glossary.

severed ties with the trans men I knew that it was possible for me to admit that I was trans. It took me a while to figure out that not all trans men fall into the one specific category of "asshole," and once I figured that out I decided to transition.

LACY

I think my coming out as gay was primarily an acknowledgment that there were other ways of doing things. "Oh that's an option?" I thought, "I'll do that instead."

My coming out was prevented by my own transphobia.[6] I struggled with stigma as well as feeling like the typical transition story didn't fit me. I wanted to be a woman, but I really didn't want to have surgery—which is common among trans men but not trans women.[7] Many trans women follow a trajectory where they take hormones, they develop breasts from the hormones, and they have a surgery to remove the penis and construct a vagina. For so long, I felt like I wasn't trans because I liked having a penis. The trans women I talked to would either tell me I wasn't trans or push me toward hormones. I kept telling them I didn't want hormones: estrogen makes your dick shrivel.

It wasn't until I met a transmasculine[8] friend that I realized a nonmedical transition was possible. We met at a soiree that a mutual friend was throwing. He was wearing a shirt that said, "Shhh! No one knows I'm a transexual."[9] I was across the room with my boyfriend when I saw him. I kept staring at this guy with half of a ladyfinger sticking out of my mouth. I was dumbstruck. When I pictured the word transexual or transvestite, I saw an image of men

6. An irrational fear or hatred of trans or gender-nonconforming people.

7. A trans woman is often a person assigned male at birth who has taken social, medical, or surgical steps to physically or socially feminize her gender expression or body. See glossary.

8. Adjective form of the term "trans man." Transfeminine is the adjective form of the term "trans woman." See glossary.

9. Often a synonym for "transgender." See glossary.

dressing as or becoming women and never the other way around. It had never really occurred to me that trans men exist, which is silly. Of course they exist!

I had a million questions for this guy. I know if some stranger asked me those same questions at a party, I would put them in their place. Lucky for me, he was very acquiescent. He explained to me that there are a lot of trans men who don't have to take hormones to pass,[10] or who don't want to take hormones, and many more who opt out of having surgery. It was the answer I had been waiting to hear. Like many other trans guys, he was a man with a vagina. Why couldn't I be a woman with a penis?

For so long I thought that surgery was a requirement for transitioning. By the end of the party, I finally understood that I could put on a feminine label despite what I wished or didn't wish to do with my genitalia. I'm twenty-seven, and I feel like I came out a little late because I only had a narrow idea of what it meant to be trans.

ERIK

During my sophomore year of college I attended an LGBT conference in Portland, Oregon. One of the sessions I went to was led by a trans man. He had been talking for about an hour before he mentioned that he was trans. I'm sure my jaw dropped down to the desk. In my entire life I had never met trans men that I was aware of. I knew several trans women for whom hormone replacement had not worked well, and I had a really stereotyped image of trans folk in my head. In an hour, this man had shattered all of my preconceived notions about transition.

I left the workshop in a daze. Downstairs, I ran into one of my friends who was also attending the conference. She immediately realized that I was in an odd mood so she suggested that we skip the next session and go for a walk. It was an unseasonably warm day for early spring, so we wandered into downtown Portland and sat on

---

10. To be perceived as one's desired gender. See glossary.

the stone steps near Chapman Square. I rambled on and on about masculinity and gender, and I finally said, "I'm just in such shock. I've never met a trans guy before."

She raised an eyebrow at me and said, "You know Kevin is trans, right?"

I had known Kevin for about six months and considered him to be a close friend. For the second time that day, my jaw dropped to the floor. I had never once suspected that Kevin might be trans. It was at that moment that I knew I was going to transition.

TAYLOR

I really think that I always wanted to be a girl. For a long time I held on to a personal fantasy that I would discover some sort of magical prism, shout a really lame catchphrase, and it would change me into a girl—Sailor Moon style. [*laughs*]

I was aware of physical transition because I'd seen transexuals on daytime TV. I blame the fact that my sister has really bad taste in television. Although, what does it say about my boredom that I didn't get up and leave the room? [*laughs*] Growing up in New Mexico, it was often too hot to go outside, so I spent a good portion of my summers in front of the TV. Even with that exposure, it somehow didn't register to me that transitioning was something that I might be able to do, and I didn't want surgery to be my gender narrative.

Eighth grade was sort of pivotal in that I privately started to experiment more with gender. I continued on this very private trajectory until my junior year of high school. I was a part of Biotech Frontiers summer program at Montana State University. The research focused on bioproduction of fuels, but while I had access to the school's library I decided to research gender. I came across a couple of different academic articles about transexuals, and it gave me a different viewpoint of the trans community that I wasn't getting from what limited media representation I saw on programs like The Jerry Springer Show. I stopped viewing trans folks as a television caricature and began to see transitioning as a possibility that might be open for me.

RUSS

I first learned about physical transition in some smutty fanfic online,[11] but I became more familiar with it when I came to college.
Once I actually understood how it worked in people's lives, the
wheels started turning.

When I first came to college I was pretty strongly set in a feminine identity. Over the course of the past three years, my identity has
taken a turn toward masculine, toward transgender. I've spent the
past year questioning whether or not I want to transition. I cross-
dress frequently, but I've never brought it up with my therapist. I'm
still trying to decide what's going to be best for me, and I don't want
a clinical lens put on my gender identity.

Information about trans issues and identities is not widely taught
in primary, secondary, or even tertiary education settings and is in-
frequently discussed in positive or realistic ways by the media. For
some, discovering vocabulary around nonbinary genders or information about transition is the first step in experimenting with gender
expression. Even when this information is known, deciding whether
or not it personally applies presents an additional barrier. Some must
also break through heavy walls of socially ingrained denial.

CATHERINE

People always ask me, "When did you know you were supposed
to be a girl?" That's not the question. The real question is, when did
I find out I wasn't?

At four, five, and six years old, I just assumed I was a girl. When
I was nine or ten I realized my feelings were starting to look permanent. We ask kids to believe in Santa Claus; believing I was a girl was
not that big of a stretch.

When I was twelve years old, I found my denial mode. I figured

---

11. "Fanfic" is short for fan fiction, which are stories about the characters or settings of an
original work, written by fans rather than by the original creator.

out how I was going to survive. Denial is the strongest force in the universe. Unfortunately, denial is single use: once it's gone, it's over.

Thirty years later, I needed to take a few continuing-education courses to keep my nurse's license valid. I took a sexuality course that was taught by a gender therapist, which was something I didn't know when I enrolled. Sitting in the class with her I realized that many of the topics hit too close to home.

I carried the phone number of that instructor around for five years. When I finally called, I said, "Hey, this is so and so. I don't know if you remember me, but I took a class from you about five years ago."

She said, "Oh, I remember *you*."

At our first appointment, she leaned forward, and where most people would say, "Now, what brought you here today?" she said, "What took you so long?"

NATALIE

If I knew I was trans at an early age, I was good at keeping myself in a state of self-denial. I clung to all things masculine. I was not rough and tumble as a young child, until the other boys began to harass me. I realized the only way I was going to get them to stop tormenting me was to take up sports.

I was probably in fifth or sixth grade when other boys started calling me a faggot, or a pansy, or a sissy, or a fairy.[12] One day after school I went into the garage and dug out an old football. I threw it as high and as far as I could and then took off running, trying to catch it before it hit the ground. This became my routine. Every day after school I would play catch by myself until the sun went down, and the next day I'd do it again. When I knew I could throw farther than the other boys in my grade, I started hanging around after school to play with them.

The first day, as they created their impromptu scrimmage teams, I

---

12. These are pejorative slurs for gay or effeminate men that are sometimes reclaimed as positive identity labels.

was picked last. The next day I was picked first. I had a great arm, and I let out all of my pent-up aggression through tackling the boys who had formerly made fun of me. I had figured out how to be masculine, and I made damned sure that no one would call me a sissy again.

Fast-forward twenty years: I was a police officer, I was married to a beautiful woman, and [I] had three kids. I was still projecting this masculine persona that I had adopted as a child. I was doing just fine in my bubble of denial until I met a woman who shattered that bubble.

I had pulled her over for a routine stop: a headlight on her car was out. As she rolled down her window, I remember thinking she was extremely attractive. I asked for her license and registration, and she handed me an ID with a man's name and picture on it. I assumed she had given me her husband's license by mistake, but when I voiced this she said, "Honey, you don't get to look like this without either selling your soul to the devil, or hiring a great plastic surgeon. I chose the latter."

I stood there gaping at her, so she assured me, "Yes, it's my ID. I got around to updating my body before I updated my license. I've got my name change and everything; I just haven't made it to the DMV."

I vaguely recall telling her that I wouldn't write her up if she promised to update her ID as soon as possible, then stumbling back to my car in a daze. My denial had been shattered by a trans woman in a Subaru.

OLIVIA

I was raised to be a devout Christian. I grew up hearing that homosexuality was a sin, that being transgender was a sin. I knew I had cross-gender feelings, but I suppressed them throughout my childhood and adolescence. As a young man, I married a woman, had two great kids, and continued to pray.

Every single night I would pray that my feelings would go away. I would pray for acceptance. I wanted to accept the fact that I was a man and that there was nothing I could do to change that.

Well, you can't say that God doesn't have a sense of humor. He blessed me with two gay kids and gave me a new understanding of what acceptance really means.

My kids came out together. My son sat his mother and me down and told us he was gay. We told him that we loved him no matter what. Then our daughter said that she was a lesbian. We laughed and joked that we'd try to love her too. They later admitted that they drew straws to decide who was going to come out first.

I couldn't stop loving my children, so I could no longer believe that homosexuality was a sin. Logically, if being gay isn't a sin, being transgender surely isn't either. I came out as trans shortly after my kids came out. It certainly wasn't the situation I had been praying for. All of those times I was praying for acceptance . . . [laughs] I guess I should have been more specific with God!

Coming Out Is a Lifelong Process

"Coming out of the closet" or just "coming out" has become common parlance for disclosing one's sexuality to others.[13] Although frequently conflated, gender identity and sexuality are two separate and distinct aspects of a person's sense of self. Gender identity describes the way a person experiences and wishes to embody their own gender, while sexuality describes to whom a person is attracted. Some transgender individuals are aware of their sexualities before they are aware of their gender identities; others are attuned to their gender identities before they have affirmed their sexualities; and others experience a change in sexual attraction as they transition.[14] Those who know they have nonheterosexual attractions before they are attuned

---

13. Sometimes "coming out" can refer to one divulging a transgender status, but often the term "disclosure" is used in reference to gender identity, while "coming out" is used in reference to sexuality. See glossary.

14. Sexuality is fluid and can change throughout one's life. For trans folk who transition hormonally, it is also possible that as hormones affect their pheromones and body chemistry, their sexual attractions shift.

to their gender identities might come out to friends or family long before they disclose trans identities.

LUIS

In high school I knew I was bisexual, but I didn't come out to my family because I knew it wasn't a safe thing to do while I still lived at home. In college I cut my hair and started presenting more masculine.

During my freshman year, I had to have surgery on my nose. When I was coming out of the anesthesia and still had IVs in my arm I said, "Mom, I'm a lesbian."

Because I was in a vulnerable position, my mom said that it was okay and that she loved me. I think she was only nice about it because we were in the hospital. After I recovered she pretended it didn't happen.

ASH

My dad had trouble with drugs, and I was removed from my home by the state. I bounced around in the foster system, stayed with friends, or stayed with people in my church until I went off to college. The summer after high school, I stayed with Mike and Amy, who volunteered at our church's youth group. They were a couple in their forties with a lot of money and no kids. They were home base for me for the first two and a half years of college.

While I was in college, I came to terms with my sexuality and my gender. I hadn't told anyone back home yet, but I really wanted to. I was terrified to tell my mom, because I had just reestablished a relationship with her. I wasn't going to tell anyone else before I got a chance to tell my mom. I was worried if someone else told her before I did, it would ruin our fragile relationship. I kept it a secret from Mike and Amy, which caused some turmoil in our relationships later on.

Even though I wasn't out to many people, I applied for a few scholarships from the Pride Foundation, a Pacific Northwest–based organization that gives scholarships to queer students. I was delighted to receive a scholarship from them, and one of my college professors decided to drive me the seventy-five miles to the scholarship banquet. I was glad I had applied, because I got a year's worth of college tuition paid for. At the awards banquet, one of the affiliates of the scholarship program took a picture of me without my knowing. A year later, that picture would get me into a lot of trouble.

During my sophomore year of college, I studied abroad in Mexico, and while I was there I was raped. I had to get all of my urgent care in a Mexican hospital, and they gave me their version of the morning-after pill, which is about three times stronger than the one you get [in the] United States. When I returned home, I had to get my six-month checkup to make sure I didn't have HIV. By the time I got back, I didn't have much money. I asked the local youth minister if he knew of any discount or free services in the area where I could get my checkup done. He took it upon himself to go to the priest and tell him that there was a student who needed a medical procedure and asked if there were any funds available. He told me he would take me to the public health clinic, which was great and I really appreciated it.

The day before we went to the clinic, he found out that I had gone to a concert and dinner with a friend upon returning from Mexico. He decided that this meant that I had money and obviously I was just squandering it and taking advantage of him. In reality, my grandparents had bought concert tickets for my best friend and me as a coming-home gift, and my friend took me out to dinner before the show because she knew I was broke. The minister took me to the public health clinic and afterward brought me back to Amy and Mike's house, where they had planned an intervention. They lectured me on fiscal responsibility. Of course, they didn't know exactly why I had needed the tests, just that I was being tested for STDs. They told me that if I were going to be making sexual decisions, I should have money set aside for the potential health costs associated with having sex. They didn't know I was a lesbian, and they didn't know I had been raped. After their horrible intervention I wasn't about to tell them.

Things were tense at home, but everything really blew up later that year, when the picture that was taken of me at the scholarship awards banquet resurfaced. Around the holidays, there is a guide distributed in the region that lists all of the nonprofits doing charitable work in the area. My picture was the stock photo for the scholarship organization, and the caption read something about giving scholarships to LGBT youth. I was holding a rainbow certificate in the picture.

Amy and Mike make a lot of money and give away a certain percentage of their income every year. While I was home over the winter break, Amy saw my picture in the nonprofit guide and started yelling and screaming, and telling me that I had betrayed her. She told me I was irresponsible and brought up the health-care incident, so I let loose and told her why I had to have those procedures in the first place. Instead of being sympathetic, she got even madder at me. She said that I should have gone to her first, and she was upset that I hadn't told her before. I thought, "Really? This is your reaction to finding out that this horrible, traumatic thing happened to me? Maybe this is why I didn't tell you I was gay."

About five months later, I stopped by to grab some things I had left at the house. Amy took me downstairs and sat me down. She basically told me that she didn't want me to come by their house ever again. She technically wasn't kicking me out because I was gay but because I hadn't told her that I was gay. What a justification.

ERIK

I knew I was gay before I even knew being transgender was an option. I was a freshman in college when I came out to my family. I sat them down, took a deep breath, and said, "I'm a lesbian."

They looked at each other and said, "Yeah, we've known for years."

I was astonished and asked how they knew. "Well," my dad said,

"I walked in on you and your girlfriend having sex when you were still in high school."

"And you never said anything?!" I asked.

My mom shrugged, "We figured you would tell us when you were ready."

"Yeah," my dad said, "we were just excited that since you were sleeping with girls, you weren't going to get knocked up." [laughs]

Disclosure of sexuality or gender identity often follows a common narrative. This sometimes-tired trajectory is a typical story line in the West and global North, and implies to a certain extent that individuals who are nonbinary or nonheterosexual are expected to explain their gender identity or sexuality to others. Many do not feel the need to disclose to others or to define themselves with labels. Others feel that disclosure is an affirming process. Ideally, everyone who wished to come out would be able to disclose their sexual orientation or gender identity in a safe environment when they are prepared to do so. However, sometimes one's sexuality or gender identity is discovered by others before there is an opportunity to disclose.

JUANITA

Coming out is a lifelong process. Everyone comes out at different times about different things. I've had to come out about my sexuality, my gender, and my HIV status, and I can't tell you which time was the hardest.

When I was in high school I knew I was gay. I knew better than to tell my parents because I knew my dad would absolutely freak out. He's ex-military and always treated me like I was at boot camp.

My younger sister and I were really close. She knew I was gay and knew to keep it a secret. One day after school I brought my boyfriend over to my house. My parents were both at work, so we took advantage of the empty house to fool around. For some reason my dad came home early. He walked into my room and caught my boyfriend and me in the act. I thought he was going to kill us. My sister had come home with him, and she shoved my dad to the floor so that my boyfriend had a chance to run. My dad stood up and clocked my sister. As I ran past them, he tried to grab me. I ducked out of the bedroom and then ran out the front door. He ran to the porch and yelled after me to never come back, so I didn't.

I caught up with my boyfriend after a few blocks. He was so mortified by what had happened that he said I couldn't stay at his house. Being the queer kid, I didn't have a lot of other friends at school, and I didn't have any place to stay.

I left the house with no money, so I walked to the mall and I checked the coin returns in all of the vending machines for change. I finally found some and used a pay phone to call my aunt. She said I could stay with her for a while.

My aunt lived thirty miles away, so I hitchhiked to her place. She let me stay on the hide-a-bed for a few weeks, but I knew she didn't really want me there. I got a job busing tables, and as soon as I got my first paycheck I bought a bus ticket to San Francisco and took off.

Expressions of sexual identity can sometimes overlap with gender identity or expression.[15] For some, sexuality is the first identity they disclose. For others, they developed and recognized their gender far before their sexualities, have no need to disclose a sexual identity, or have a sexual identity that overlaps with a nonbinary gender identity.

SETH

I dropped out of Williams College when I discovered Northampton, Massachusetts. It was the first place I ever saw dykes. That was the first time in my life that I saw anyone who looked like me. I was nineteen or twenty, and I quit Williams to move there.

When I moved to Northampton, I was still really shy. I didn't quite know how to interact with people because I had been so isolated. I

---

15. For example, aggressive, butch, stud, fairy, and fae identities often involve both sexuality and gender components. See glossary.

got a job working on the street in front of a leather upholstery store where the manager of the store taught me how to shine shoes. He had this big block with nice brass footrests and a huge leather upholstered chair sitting on it. It was supposed to draw attention to the store, but the lines of people were there to see me. The Harley motorcycle riders, the Smith college students, and the other local dykes would line up, and I would shine their shoes. My name in the town basically became Shoe-Shine Boy. People whose boots I was shining would ask me my name and how old I was, and when I would tell them that I was in my twenties they would just laugh because I passed as a twelve-year-old boy. That was really my first genderqueer identity: I was a shoe-shine boy. I was not only genderqueer, but I was also agequeer, which is a term for those of us who pass as indeterminate ages. No one could tell how old I was or what gender I was. They just knew I was Seth the Shoe-Shine Boy.

Shining shoes was how I learned to socialize. I could look at a customer's feet while talking to him or her. I was too shy to look at a face, but I started gradually learning how to interact socially by doing this. Having this genderqueer identity helped me learn how to operate socially in a weird way. Since no one exactly knew how I was supposed to act, I had the opportunity to experiment. Through these foot-focused conversations, I started making friends with dykes. It took me about four years of shining shoes, but gradually I started making real friends and dating.

KURTIS

Learning the word "transgender" was vital for me. Once I had the vocabulary, I had something tangible I could search for. I spent hours locked alone in my mom's office searching for information about transition on the Internet. I joined every online chat group and forum for trans folk that I could find, just looking for resources and trying to get the courage to tell my family that I wanted to be a boy.

Because I was so young, a lot of people on the forums encouraged me not to transition. Many of them had faced familial rejection, so they tried to convince me to wait until I had graduated from high school before telling my family. I wanted to start transition as soon as possible, but for a minor it is necessary to have parental permission to pursue any type of medical treatment. For me to transition, my family had to be on board.

One person in the forums tried to convince me to come out as a lesbian before coming out as trans. He said it would be easier for my family to wrap their heads around, and they were less likely to reject me.

I had spent so much time contemplating my gender that I had never stopped to think about my sexuality. I didn't want to tell my family I was a lesbian because I wasn't sure whether or not I was. I had no idea who I wanted to date: I just knew I wanted to be a boy.

Disclosing a Trans Identity: I Had to Take a Stand

Disclosing a trans identity can be just as difficult, if not more so, than coming out. While there has been some media exposure on issues of gay, lesbian, and even bisexual sexualities, relatively little accurate information exists in popular media about trans identities. Disclosing and explaining a trans identity to significant others, family, or friends can be a difficult undertaking.

CATHERINE

I was at the beach one February day. The wind was howling, and I was putting on my wetsuit to go surfing. In the morning there are always a large number of old people walking the beaches. As I was pulling on my wetsuit, I felt a touch on my arm. There was a tiny old lady looking up into my face. She asked, "Are you a boy or a girl?"

Dumbfounded, I said, "I don't have a good answer for that."

She said, "Oh," and just kept on walking. I stood there in the wind, watching her go.

Interactions like that stopped when I started wearing women's clothing. People stopped giving me a hard time. People stopped staring at me and making comments, which they frequently did before. No longer did little old ladies come up to me on the beach and question my gender. The first day I put on a dress was the day I finally got to disappear.

DAKOTA

I mostly disclosed just to close friends at first. I kept information about my identity pretty close to the vest for a long time. I had some conflict with my mother about being gender transgressive, which I think really contributed to me not wanting to come out. I was twenty the first time that my mother and I had a discussion about my gender. She took me clothes shopping for a family event, and I told her I wanted to wear a suit. When she asked why, I told her that I didn't really feel like a girl. She flipped out and told me that I was making my feelings up, which was really invalidating. I didn't bring it up with her again for years.

When I was twenty-six, I was in a job environment where I worked with a lot of women. I was grouped in with them all the time. Even though I was quite androgynous, people assumed that because I was around women I must be a woman, too. Every day, someone would say, "Good morning, ladies!" or, "Can you gals take a look at this?" or, "What's new, girls?"

One day I couldn't stand it, so I finally came out to all of my colleagues. Unlike coming out to my mother, it went really well. I work in the college of nursing, so there were a lot of health-care professionals who really got it.

Last year, I decided to start pursuing surgeries, and I had to take a stand with my mother at that point. Either she could choose to be a part of my transition or she could choose to continue ignoring me. I guess she realized that I was serious, so she has finally come around a bit. She's not thrilled, but at least she's started talking to me again.

LUIS

During my sophomore year, my dad asked me if I was trans. I told him no. I wasn't sure whether or not I was trans, and I wasn't ready to discuss it with him. My dad is a tyrant. He's emotionally abusive, so I knew he wasn't asking out of love or compassion.

When I told my mom I was trans, she freaked out and said, "I've cried so many tears for you, I don't think I'll have any left for my mother's funeral."

It's very dramatic, but she's from Colombia; that's just how she talks. Her words are always so descriptive and very tragically poetic. The next time my mom and I talked on the phone, it was like it didn't happen at all. She just ignored it.

However, when I've spoken with her recently I mentioned that I'm going to have to come out to Papi, and she said, "He'll just have to get over it."

This seems like progress, but at the same time my mom hasn't switched pronouns for me yet. I don't ever expect my mother to call me mijo instead of mija.[16]

WILSON

I was nine when my parents split up and ten when they actually divorced. My dad came to visit me for the first year but then he moved to his girlfriend's house three hours away. After he moved he said he'd come visit on Thursdays, but he didn't do that for very long, and now I don't see him at all. The last time I saw him I was at a play my sister was in. He never comes to any of mine, although I don't know why, because he always comes to my brother's plays. I guess he stopped coming to my plays after my mom told him I was trans. He didn't come to my brother's last play because I was also in it.

We talk on the phone sometimes, but I don't have a relationship with him at all. He asked me yesterday if I was sure I wanted to go on

---

16. *Mijo* is a colloquial expression combining the Spanish words *mí* (my) and *hijo* (son). *Mija* means "my daughter."

hormones. I told him that I wanted to go on hormones since I was four. I would've known sooner, but I didn't have the words to express it yet. My parents made me wear dresses until I was four, and that's when I could finally tell him I didn't want to wear dresses. I didn't know anything about hormones until I was much older, and once I found out about transitioning I knew that's what I wanted to do.

If I were living with my dad, I still wouldn't have come out yet because he's such a homophobe. I have such phobic nightmares about him. I dreamed last night that my mom died, and I had to go live with my dad. I was screaming and crying and I didn't want to go. It was a really terrible nightmare, and that was just from talking to him on the phone yesterday.

KURTIS

It took me a few months between finding the *Teen People* article about transgender youth and actually disclosing my trans identity to my family. My parents divorced when I was two months old, so my mom was the person I had to tell. One day, I told her that I needed to talk to her.

She sat down on the couch and waited in silence. I don't know what was going through her head, but she must have known that my confession was going to be a big one, because she didn't say anything. It took me nearly an hour before I finally said, "I'm a boy. I want to be a boy."

She said, "Okay. Where do we go from here?"

I was so relieved. I had no idea what the next steps would be, but the fact that she was willing to support me was huge. There was definitely a learning curve for her, and in the coming years she wasn't always the best advocate, but she was willing to support me and that was monumental.

LACY

I definitely felt forced to disclose. I got to that point where I felt like I couldn't live without disclosing. I was in a very emotionally turbulent place, and I was floundering in my relationships too. I couldn't reach out to people because I didn't know what was wrong. I knew that I was getting into the danger zone otherwise known as "suicide alley." I came to a fork in the road: either I come out, or I let these suicidal thoughts take over. That's really what propelled me to start admitting that I wasn't cisgender.[17]

Coming out as a fae[18] man was more significant emotionally for me than coming out as gay, because it was really who I was. I struggled a bit more with it, because there were higher stakes and because it's not a very common identity. I had very few examples where I could point out what it meant to be fae. I don't fall into the typical trans narrative—and really, the more you talk to people you realize that there isn't one. I liked looking pretty, but I didn't mind masculine things when I was growing up. That made it really hard for me to come out: I constantly felt like I was hearing one specific narrative of how trans women come out and it didn't apply to me.

My nuclear family is just my dad. I'm an only child, and I lost my mom when I was nine. There's an interesting dynamic that happens between my dad and me. Both of us really deeply understand that we are each other's only family so we gotta work shit out. I know it's been hard for my dad to wrap his head around the idea that I'm a woman who wants to keep her penis, but I can see him doing hard work to figure this whole thing out.

JAIME

Both of my parents were really abusive growing up. I'm the second of four kids, and I was the first kid to leave the house when I was nineteen. It was a matter of survival for me. After I moved out, I tried setting boundaries with my parents about how much communication they could have with me. They couldn't respect any of my boundaries so eventually I just cut off all communication with them.

17. Term for a person who identifies with the gender they were assigned at birth. See glossary.

18. Usually means an extremely effeminate gay man. See glossary.

About nine months after that, my father started stalking me and I was extremely concerned that he was going to injure me. The police got involved and told him that he would be arrested if he bothered me again. It's been about a year and a half since that incident, and I haven't spoken to my parents or told them about my transition.

My next youngest sibling is an auto mechanic. To call that field aggressively gendered would be an understatement. He's gone the same evangelical direction as my parents, so he's pretty homophobic, which has caused a lot of tension between us.

I'm very good friends with my older sister. She also identifies as queer, and she's still trying to figure out her own gender identity, so she's been a fantastic support. When I started my transition, I sent her lists of names to see which she liked better. It's been awesome to have someone to talk to, especially since I can't really talk to my parents or brother.

QUINN

Disclosing my trans identity to my family was a process. I'm the youngest of five kids. Most of my siblings are married and have their own kids now. I'm not good at math, but that's a lot of people to tell.

The first person I came out to was my next oldest sister. She and I have always been close, which made her both the easiest and the hardest person to tell. I don't think I've been more scared of anything in my life. I told her over the phone, and she was a little surprised but was very supportive. I don't remember anything about the conversation except an overwhelming feeling of relief. I don't know how to describe what happened afterward. Whatever the opposite of a panic attack is, that's what I had. I flopped down on my bed on my face and couldn't move. My housemate came home and thought I was injured. She rushed over to me shouting, "What's wrong!? Are you okay?"

"I just got steamrolled by happiness," I told her.

I was more nervous about telling my parents, so I wrote both of my parents a letter and gave it to them over dinner. They were receptive to the letters. My dad doesn't really communicate much of anything, but I thought it would be mean to give my mom a letter and not him. My mom told me she supported me no matter what, but she hasn't really followed through with that sentiment. My dad just avoids me.

Luckily, the rest of my siblings have been fantastic, and they call my parents out whenever they misgender[19] me or say something ignorant or offensive.

CAMERON

When I told my parents I was transitioning they definitely never stopped supporting me, which I never really had a fear of, but they weren't exactly great about it. When I came out as bisexual in high school my mom told me it was a phase. I didn't really get the warm fuzzies from her, so I didn't really talk about it. I came out as a lesbian in college, and my dad freaked out. He started sending me really nasty typewritten letters in the mail, with the theme of, "I know what's good for you. You shouldn't be doing this. You're not employable."

When I came out as trans, it took my parents a longer time to understand what was going on. They are pretty liberal people. Still, I don't think I was really prepared for how long it would take them to understand what I was really talking about. They are a little older, and they didn't have any experience at all with trans people before me. It's been emotional, but it hasn't really caused any true turmoil. I'm an only child, so they're kind of stuck with me. They call me "Cam" all the time, but they haven't really got the hang of using male pronouns yet. They're good, but they're not perfect.

HUGO

My family is an old-school Portuguese fishing family. Since my parents divorced, it seems that the two sides of my family are at

---

19. To use a name or pronouns other than those preferred by the person in question.

extremes. When I finally admitted I was trans to my family, I lost all but three members. My mother and my two sisters still talk to me, but my stepmother threatened to shoot me. She didn't react well at all.

Most of the businesses around Provincetown are family owned. Two days after I said I was going to start hormones, my father sat me down and said, "We can't do this any more."

That was his way of firing me. He wouldn't say "you're out of the family," but I was kicked out of the house. They insisted they needed my room for the person they hired to replace me. I worked for them about eighty hours per week, six months out of the year. Their whole lives revolve around fishing, and if I can't be involved in the business I'm not a part of their lives.

This came about in part because my stepmother wasn't comfortable with my transition. She basically gave my father an ultimatum and said, "You have to choose between your child and me."

He chose her.

Due to the fear (and all-too-frequent reality) of rejection or violence, disclosing a trans identity to parents and siblings can be a complicated undertaking. When a person is married or has children, disclosure has the potential to jeopardize or complicate additional relationships.

BELLA

The fights would start any time my wife and I had to get dressed up to go somewhere: weddings, funerals, and graduations; they were all sources of contention between us. It took me years to pin down exactly why I became haughty and angry around these events.

I became moody as we were getting ready, sullen in the car, and by the time we arrived I was a real ass. For the longest time I just thought I was antisocial.

My wife was the one who figured out what the problem was. We had never talked about the possibility of me transitioning. I had never once brought up my cross-gender feelings in all of the years we had been together. Yet somehow she knew exactly what I had been battling in my head my entire life. We were getting ready for a friend's wedding, and I started my routine of pouting. The groom was a navy buddy of mine, and I was expected to wear my old navy uniform. My wife came up to me, laid her hand on my arm, and said, "You only have to wear it for a little while."

That was the moment when I realized why these events made me so angry. I was jealous that all of the women got to wear beautiful, sparkling dresses and I was stuck in a suit or a tux. First of all, it wasn't fair that I had to wear a cummerbund, and second, those dresses would have looked better on me! [laughs]

My wife was so compassionate and understood my anger and dysphoria better than I did. I put on my navy uniform, and we went out. It was the most fun I've ever had at a wedding because I knew that my uniform was just a costume that I had to wear for a few hours; it wasn't who I really was.

When we got home that night, my wife asked, "Of all the dresses we saw tonight, which one do you think would look best on you?"

I replied in the shakiest voice, "The mauve cocktail dress that Charla was wearing."

And she simply smiled and said, "That's the one I was thinking too! Think we ought to get you one?"

I hugged my wife, and we both cried for hours. So many marriages end when one partner transitions, but my marriage became stronger. There are no more secrets between us.

WENDY

My wife and I had been married for twenty-three years before I told her I wanted to be a woman. During that entire time, I never once dressed or undressed in front of her. That's not an easy feat to maintain for twenty-three years.

I was ashamed of my body. I could barely look at myself, let alone have anyone else look at me. I was always partially clothed during intimacy.

It was so difficult to want to have sex. I was attracted to my wife, but I hated my body so much. Every time I became aroused, I was disgusted with my body so I wouldn't want to be intimate. My wife thought I wasn't attracted to her and felt bad about herself.

One evening we were arguing about the frequency (or lack thereof) of our intimacy. She blamed herself. She said we weren't intimate because she wasn't attractive. I couldn't let her carry on thinking that.

"You're beautiful," I told her. "I don't want to make love because I hate my body. Every time we go at it I'm reminded that I'm a man, and I don't want to be a man anymore."

She definitely realized the problem wasn't her. But she also realized she didn't want to be married to a freak. It wasn't long after that conversation that she filed for divorce.

NATALIE

My wife walked in on me wearing one of her dresses. She went out shopping for the day, and while she was out of the house I took the liberty of trying on some of her makeup, jewelry, and clothing. She had only been gone for about thirty minutes when I heard the front door open. I panicked and looked around desperately for a place to hide, but she walked into the bedroom before I had moved a muscle.

She stood, framed in the doorway, staring at me. I was too terrified to speak. I just knew she was going to leave me, file for divorce, get custody of the kids, and move out of state. To my great disbelief, she tilted her head and said, "I forgot my purse . . . and your eye shadow is ridiculously uneven."

Then she began laughing a joyful, wondrous laugh. She laughed so hard I couldn't help but laugh with her. She sat down next to me on the bed and said, "This is it, isn't it? I always knew that behind all of your deep, brooding masculinity there was something you were stifling. Is this it? Is this the 'dreadful secret' you've always kept hidden?"

I nodded. She asked, "Is it that you like to wear women's clothing, or that you want to be a woman?"

In the smallest squeak of a voice, I whispered for the first time in my life, "I want to be a woman."

My wife stood up, grabbed her purse, and laughed, "Good! I was always concerned that you were hiding something terrible! I'm going back out shopping now that I have my purse. Need me to pick you up any more costume jewelry?"

Before she left she touched my shoulder and smiled at me. I knew her gentle teasing was her way of telling me that she still loved me no matter what. When she left, I cried tears of relief for hours.

I've Never Heard of Anyone's
Transition Experience Being Easy

Transition is a personal and nuanced experience, and there is no standard definition of the word. Social transitions often (but not always) include asking others to use one's preferred name and pronouns, as well as expressing gender outwardly in a way that reflects one's internal identity.

Medical transitions can include hormone replacement therapy, during which a person takes cross-sex hormones to alter their secondary-sex characteristics.[1] Female-to-male individuals often take testosterone to achieve masculinizing effects. Male-to-female individuals often take estrogen along with additional medications to block testosterone production in order to achieve feminizing effects. Surgical options are numerous and varied. Gender-confirmation surgery is a recent umbrella term that encompasses all surgical procedures intended to affirm one's desired gender. Many male-to-female individuals will have genital-reassignment surgery. Many female-to-male individuals will undergo breast removal but avoid genital-reassignment surgery. Some will transition socially but not medically. Others (especially genderqueer or gender-nonconforming individuals) will have surgeries without hormones, or vice versa.

Medically transitioning is a time-consuming and costly process, but many feel medical transition is necessary in order to express their

---

1. See "hormone replacement therapy" in the medical glossary.

gender in the ways that are most authentic to them. In fact, there has been a body of medical research on the mental-health benefits of transition.[2]

WENDY

When I was a kid, I learned to read at a really early age.[3] I read anything and everything I could get my hands on. Even though I didn't consciously realize it, I was desperately searching through literature to find any glimpse of other people who were like me. It wasn't until I was an adult that I found what I was looking for. When I was a kid, we barely had TV, and there certainly weren't transgender people on it! There weren't books about transitioning, and there was no Internet. As an adult, I've been able to find all of the information I couldn't find as a kid. The last forty years have produced all kinds of history and medical books about trans people. That's important to me because I'm still looking to find myself in history. What's amazing is that all of this information about trans history has been carefully and painstakingly archived, but younger generations of trans folk just don't seem to care about it. If you ask them who Christine Jorgensen was, they'll stare at you with blank faces.

I talk about history a lot, because it's something that everyone needs to be aware of. People think that transgender people are a new phenomena, but we've always been around. Trans folk really started appearing, in the way that we think of transgender and transsexual people today, around the 1950s. I'm old enough to remember hearing a lot about Christine Jorgensen when I was a kid. At the time I didn't think much about it, but looking back, it's clear to me that her transition was an incredibly important moment in trans

---

2. See Eli Coleman, Walter Bockting, Marsha Botzer, et al., *Standards of Care for the Health of Transsexual, Transgender, and Gender-Nonconforming People,* 7th version (Minneapolis: World Professional Association for Transgender Health, 2012), or the *DSM-V* entry on gender dysphoria for more information.
3. Wendy is a trans-history buff and agreed to provide a brief synopsis of the history of transgender medicine.

history. Of course, there were other transgender people before her, but none of them got much media attention. Jorgensen was one of the first trans women to come to the national spotlight. The idea of a medical transition certainly existed, but that was the first time that anyone in the public eye had transitioned so successfully. She was sensationalized by all of the news outlets. She had been a GI during the war, so it was even more shocking when she became a woman.

Jorgensen's doctor, Harry Benjamin, helped to set up many of the medical precedents that would affect trans people later on. Benjamin was an endocrinologist, and he worked with Jorgensen to get her an estrogen prescription. Once Jorgensen became a media sensation, all of these trans people around the country started writing to her and Benjamin to ask about estrogen, to ask about testosterone. They never talked about that part on the news, though. They painted Jorgensen as one in a million, so it didn't occur to me as a kid that transitioning might have been an option for me too. It never occurred to me that there were any other people like her, or that I might be like her.

When Harry Benjamin realized the astounding number of people who had similar feelings and desires as Jorgensen, he started working with other doctors and endocrinologists to come up with some guidelines for working with the transgender community. These became known as the Standards of Care. At that time, there were none. In the 1950s and '60s, these guidelines were really quite progressive. However, they haven't been updated as much as they perhaps should be, and now they can be quite a hindrance to people who are trying to transition.

Interestingly, these guidelines came out before 1978. Seventy-eight is important because it is the year that homosexuality was declassified as a mental disorder in the DSM. Gay and lesbian activists petitioned and protested until homosexuality was removed from the DSM. As with a lot of organizing that happened in those days, they threw trans folks under the bus. They were successful in taking homosexuality out of the DSM but instead we got gender identity disorder.[4]

Even though homosexuality was removed from the DSM, homophobia ran rampant in those days. It still does but not to the same extent as it did in the seventies. At that time, transitioning was viewed as a "cure" for homosexuality. Transition was permitted, as long as the person would be heterosexual in their new gender. Some people still transition to become heterosexual, but more and more, people are remaining queer after transition, or are becoming queer because of transition.[5] Previously, trans women were only allowed to transition so that they wouldn't be seen as homosexuals. Trans men disappeared altogether: they went on to have wives and families, and they were able to completely erase themselves from the transgender community. We lost a lot of would-be allies that way.

Gender identity disorder was the diagnosis that every trans person had to have in order to medically transition. You still have to have a diagnosis, but they recently changed the name to gender dysphoria[6] to soften the stigma. You are required to go to a psychologist or psychiatrist for an arbitrary number of sessions in order to convince that person that you have gender identity disorder. Once the mental-health professional is completely convinced that you really are transgender, they will write you a letter that you can take to an endocrinologist, who will then prescribe you hormones if you are in good health and have the means to pay for it. Without this letter you will get nowhere.

As Wendy outlined, Harry Benjamin was one of the first-known endocrinologists in the United States to prescribe hormone replacement

---

4. Gender identity disorder was changed to gender dysphoria in the fifth edition of the *DSM*. See glossary.
5. That is, if a man is heterosexual prior to transition, that same person would be considered a lesbian woman after transitioning. If a woman is heterosexual prior to transition, that same person would be considered a gay man after transitioning.
6. The official diagnosis that trans folk have to obtain from a mental-health practitioner in order to access hormones or surgeries through the Standards of Care.

therapy for trans patients. He had a growing number of patients seeking hormones prior to becoming Christine Jorgensen's physician, but her media exposure undoubtedly led to greater awareness of medical transition. The Harry Benjamin International Gender Dysphoria Association (renamed World Professional Association for Transgender Health [WPATH] in 2006) adopted the first recommendations for working with trans patients. The *Standards of Care for the Health of Transsexual, Transgender, and Gender-Nonconforming People* is now in its seventh version and is considered the standard guideline for providing medical and mental health care for trans folk.[7]

Gender identity disorder was included in the *DSM-III* for the first time in 1980. This entry included coding for listing the patient's prior sexual history (heterosexual, homosexual, or asexual). While some mental-health providers and physicians were more likely to provide transitional care for patients who would be heterosexual after transition, trans folk consistently embodied a wide variety of sexual identities. As Wendy asserted, some trans folk certainly went stealth[8] after transition, but there are many who remained or became integrally involved in trans rights and other activist endeavors.

FELIPE

When I figured out I was trans, I went to my college's counseling center to begin the therapy process. I was trying to deal with my family, who were not excited about the prospect of me transitioning. They were providing all of my financial support while I got my degree, and I wasn't going to shun their support for a hairy chest. I could have had my letter within six months, but I waited for nearly

---

7. However, it should be noted that alternative models for treating trans patients exist and include the Health Law Standards of Care for Transsexualism and the Informed Consent for Access to Trans Health model, both of which rely on informed consent and open dialogue between patients and providers.

8. When a trans person is consistently perceived by others as their desired gender and actively chooses not to disclose their transgender status to anyone. See glossary.

three years before I asked my counselor to write it. By that point, I was about to graduate and my family had finally realized I wasn't backing down.

LUIS

I was already seeing a counselor when I decided I was going to transition. I had always been very open with her, so when I came out to her she said it made sense. She wasn't at all surprised. I was the first trans person that she had ever seen, but she's really been working on getting educated. From the time I came out to when I started hormones only took three months. That's like, a shit ton of privilege. I've never heard of anyone's transition experience being easy. I was so surprised.

Historically, the Standards of Care for youth have been much more stringent than they are for adults. Not having reached the age of consent, it has long been required that youth obtain parental permission to receive transitional care, participate in individual and family counseling, and experience the onset of puberty in their original sex. With the increased use of GnRH analogues,[9] many trans youth are now able to delay puberty while fulfilling the mental-health and medical evaluations for transition. While the restrictions on youth transition are slowly easing, there are many trans adults who had to adhere to the more stringent requirements as youth and without the aid of puberty-delaying hormones.

KURTIS

By the time I came out to my mom, I was more than ready to transition. Living in a rural area in the early 2000s, people weren't exactly versed in trans care. I had to see a pediatric gender therapist who made me undergo the two years of hell known as the "real life

---

9. Medication used to suppress puberty in youth. See glossary.

experience."[10] During this time you are not allowed to be on hormones but are supposed to live your life in your desired gender in order to "prove" that you won't change your mind. I was a fifteen-year-old with a soprano speaking voice and I was supposed to dress, act, and comport myself as a man. I looked boyish enough, but as soon as I opened my mouth everyone knew that I was a girl. I had terrible participation grades in high school because I was terrified to speak during class. When my classmates did find out that I wasn't the boy they assumed I was, I faced bullying, harassment, and ridicule. I had to transfer high schools twice.

At that time, no one was really sure what to do with youth who wanted to transition. The Standards of Care said I could start hormones when I was sixteen but only with parental consent. These were guidelines that are meant to be adjusted on a case-by-case basis, but my counselor followed them as a strict set of rules. After two years of living full time as a boy without the aid of hormone therapy I was at a breaking point. I finally told my counselor that I had done everything she wanted without complaint and it was time for her to write me my damn letter. By that time I was nearly eighteen anyway.

BELLA

I'm wary of psychiatrists and the mental-health abuses that they have forced on African Americans in particular. I knew I wanted to start taking estrogen, so I went to my doctor and told him. He told me all about the Standards of Care and outlined the whole excruciating process for me. When he got to the part about seeing a shrink, I must have made a terrible face, because he stopped and put his hand on my shoulder before continuing.

If I had to see a shrink, it was very important to me to see someone who was African American. I talked to friends and coworkers to

---

10. The real life experience required individuals seeking medical transition to live full time in the gender to which they intended to transition for a set duration of time before becoming eligible for hormone replacement therapy or genital-reassignment surgery.

find names of psychs. I would call each one up and ask them if they knew anything about gender-identity issues. It took a few weeks, but I finally found a woman who was willing to see me.

The first time I went into her office I was nervous. There is a stigma in going to a shrink. I sat down and I told her, "I don't want to talk about my feelings. I'm a woman. I know I'm a woman, but my doctor says he needs a letter from you to prove it."

She leaned back and said, "Your doctor just wants to make sure you're not going to sue him later. You can't blame him for covering his ass."

That made me laugh out loud. I was much more comfortable with her from then on. I talked to her about a lot of feelings I didn't know I had and about a lot of things from when I was in the navy. Even though she wrote me my transition letter years ago, I still see her.

Trans Folk Are Not That Hard to Treat

Factors such as age, education, HIV status, and socioeconomic class inform who has access to transition-related medical care and how these services are accessed, if at all.

WILSON

I'll be sixteen next January. If I don't get testosterone right when I'm sixteen, people are going to say, "You're a girl because you have a girl voice. You're that old?"

I'm just going to get on T [testosterone] as fast as possible.

VICKY

There aren't many doctors who are willing to treat you if you're trans and have a disability. It took ages to find a trans-friendly primary care physician [PCP]. I have epilepsy, so now I have to worry about finding a trans-friendly neurologist. My PCP recommended a neurologist who had a terrible bedside manner. I didn't feel safe with him, so I don't really know what to do because my PCP is concerned that starting me on estrogen will change my seizure threshold. It's like my transition is being held ransom until I can find a trans-competent neurologist.

KURTIS

My doctor didn't want to put me on any sort of hormones until I turned eighteen. I finally forced him to give me hormones when I was seventeen and a half. It was a battle to get the letter from my therapist and another battle to get my doctor to write the prescription. I had to see a pediatric endocrinologist in Portland, which was a six-hour drive. Every time I went to see him he insisted that he perform a gynecological exam. I wasn't sexually active, so it was always very traumatic.

I finally blew up at him and my mom. I had played their games, jumped through their hoops, and more than demonstrated I wasn't going to change my mind. I was nearly eighteen, and I wasn't going to let them deter me for an additional six months so that I could make the decision myself. I had already made the decision long ago.

SUPRIYA

I transitioned thirteen years ago, and it was harder to find care then. We act as though transitioning is this new and novel thing, but really the science has been around since the 1950s. More and more endocrinologists and primary care providers are realizing that trans folk are not that hard to treat. Media attention and advocacy groups have made transitioning much more mainstream. Now we have people like Laverne Cox, who is a role model and advocate, and so many people know who she is. Fifteen years ago all we had was Jerry Springer, and that wasn't really something I could relate to.

This generation of trans youth, and youth with supportive families, have more flexibility than ever in accessing transition-related medical and mental-health care. However, lack of insurance coverage, financial hardship, or a lack of parental consent can still bar youth from accessing care.

KELLY

I came out to my family when I was twelve. Luckily, my moms are lesbians, so not only were they unsurprised by my revelation [but] they were also really supportive. Being a part of the LGBT community, they already knew trans women who could point them in the right direction.

I am one of those extremely lucky people who came out before I started puberty. My moms pushed really hard for me to be able to take puberty-suppressing hormones.[11] Basically, hormone blockers just give trans youth a medication that tells your body to press pause on puberty. Once you've met the other therapy requirements, you can start taking estrogen or testosterone and go through puberty as your desired sex rather than your biological sex. The Standards of Care suggest that youth wait until they are sixteen to start taking testosterone or estrogen, but my moms convinced my doctor to let me start taking estrogen when I was fourteen.

I am one of those very rare trans women who hasn't had to have surgery in order to pass. I never went through puberty as a boy so I didn't get that tall, my shoulders aren't wide, I don't have an Adam's apple, and I never got hairy. Most trans women are fighting against all of the effects of having gone through puberty, so they have to take estrogen along with other testosterone-blocking medications.[12] Many of them will have their tracheas shaved to reduce the size of their Adam's apples. I never had to have electrolysis because I didn't have a beard. I never had to go to voice coaching because my voice never dropped. Come to think of it, neither did anything else! [laughs]

---

11. See "GnRH analogues" in the glossary.

12. Antiandrogens serve to suppress testosterone, while progestins help to enhance the feminizing effects of estrogen. One or more of these medications might be prescribed in conjunction with estrogen.

FELIPE

In Alaska it can be really difficult for trans people to get medical care. I get my T through a mail-order pharmacy, but I have to see a doctor to have my prescription renewed every six months.

There is an LGBT office in downtown Anchorage, but they have absolutely no trans resources. They weren't able to help me find a doctor, so I called my insurance company and asked them to find me an endocrinologist in my area who was covered. I went through the list of endocrinologists that they gave me and started calling all of them to find someone who was willing to treat me.

ERIK

It's true what they say about being afraid of things that aren't understood. I was walking down the street and some punk teen came up to me and asked, "So, what are you?" It wasn't the first time. I've been spit on, called names, chased. Before I was on hormones, the threat of violence was always present. Starting hormones is so exciting because it's like being born again — as the correct gender. I think every trans person counts down the days until they get on hormones. My counselor wrote a letter on my behalf in August and then sent it to the endocrinologist. I made an appointment as soon as the letter was sent, but the doctor was booked until the end of September.

The day of my appointment, I was so excited that I got to the doctor's office forty-five minutes early, just in case she had a cancellation. The exam itself was routine. She wrote me a prescription for testosterone and told me that once I got it filled I could come back and the nurse would administer it for me. It was about 4:30 and the office closed at 5:00. I was bound and determined to see the nurse that afternoon so I rushed across town to the pharmacy; then I rushed back to the office. It was 4:58 when I got back. I ran into the office, out of breath, and the nurse just shook her head and laughed. She pulled me into the back room and told me to drop my pants. So there I was, sitting on the exam table with my pants around my ankles, shaking like a leaf. I was so excited but so nervous too! She showed me the spot on my thigh where the injection should go and asked if I wanted to do it myself. I told her I was terrified of needles. She shook her head and laughed again and told me I was in for a tough road. She was right.

The typical dosage for injectable testosterone is one milliliter every two weeks. Two weeks later I needed another dose, but I was on my own. I paid for everything out of pocket, so I couldn't afford to have the nurse give me injections twice a month.

I was extremely nervous about giving myself an injection. I had pulled the testosterone into the syringe and I was sitting in my boxers at the kitchen table. My girlfriend made me a Black Russian to ease my nerves, but it wasn't working. I realized I didn't know how hard I should jab myself with the needle. I didn't want to hurt myself, but I also didn't want the needle to get stuck half way in and have to do it twice. I asked my girlfriend to give me the injection and she politely told me where that needle could go.

After another Black Russian, I called my best friend and asked him to come over. When he arrived I made him a drink and asked him if he would give me the injection. He likewise said no. We spent the next half hour making our way through my bottle of vodka, and I still hadn't gotten the courage to stab that damn needle into my leg. My friend was getting tired of my cowardice and he offered to let me do a practice run on him. Everyone needs a friend like that. He dropped his pants, and I jabbed a clean needle right into his thigh. I don't know who was more horrified: him, me, or my girlfriend. Anyways, he told me that since he was brave enough, and since I had practiced once, it was time for me to give myself the injection. At that point I was pretty drunk and out of excuses, so I did it, and as it turned out, it wasn't too bad.

TAYLOR

I knew I was going to transition when I went to college. I arrived at Washington State University about a week before classes started my freshman year. My mom helped me get settled in, and as soon as she left, I went to the campus Gender Identity/Expression and Sexual Orientation Resource Center [GIESORC]. I had been e-mailing the director of GIESORC for months beforehand to get any information she could give me about resources for trans people. I was living in an all-male dorm, but by that point it was too late to do anything about my room and board because it was pretty well restricted. However, the director helped me get in touch with a psychologist at the university counseling center who had worked with trans people in the past.

After a few visits my therapist asked me if I wanted to have her refer me to a doctor for hormones. I actually said no because I really wanted to make sure I had legitimately followed the Standards of Care, so I waited three months to get to the referral. I was paranoid that I'd come up against somebody later down the line who would deny me surgery because I hadn't followed the standards to the letter. I wanted my transition to be seen as legitimate as possible to all the gatekeepers along the path, so I adhered to the standards pretty anally.

I got my prescription for hormones sometime in November. I was prescribed two medications: estrodial, which I still take today, and medroxyprogesterone.[13] To this day I'm still not 100 percent sure what medroxyprogesterone did for me as far as the transition process is concerned. After I picked up the pills from the pharmacy, I waited a whole month before I took them. I was excited, but I was also terrified. So I waited until Christmas Day to take them. As it turned out I had nothing to be worried about. Starting estrogen was great, not just for the feminizing effects but also for decreasing my sex drive. Having fewer erections was fantastic.

Although following the Standards of Care is the prescribed method of obtaining hormones, not everyone transitions through this method.

---

13. Estrodial is an oral, topical, or injectable form of estrogen. Medroxyprogesterone is a progestin.

Education, distrust of medical or mental-health practitioners, fear of having a clinical lens put on one's gender, and the expense of seeking mental and physical health care are a few of many factors that inform who transitions via the channels outlined in the Standards of Care.

JUANITA

I've been an addict since I was nineteen. Even though I had insurance and could afford counseling, no therapist was going to write me a letter to transition. I knew I was trans 'cause I'd talked to other trannies,[14] but when they told me about going to therapy I was really depressed. I knew it was never going to happen for me.

For a long time I worked cleaning houses for rich white people. [laughs] It was a living, and it fed my addictions. In every house I was assigned, I would go on an Easter egg hunt: I'd look through their cabinets and drawers and nightstands to find painkillers. Usually, I'd be able to find old supplies of dillies,[15] oxy,[16] addies,[17] you name it. As long as I only nabbed one or two at a time, people never figured it out. Once in a while someone would get fired for stealing money or jewelry. I never stole anything other than pills.

I was working for this old lady who must have been going through the change, because she had all of these bottles of estrogen pills in her bathroom. That was the first and only time I stole the whole bottle.

I started taking those pills every day until I ran out. It was a huge bottle, so it lasted a few months. I was amazed how quickly I formed breasts from just those little pills. I never had much in the way of facial hair, so it was pretty easy for me to walk around without getting clocked. When I ran out of pills, I put on a bra and a dress and I went down to the free clinic to ask for more.

The doctor asked me if I had a letter from a therapist. I told her

---

14. Pejorative term sometimes reclaimed by trans women. See glossary.
15. Dilaudid, a painkiller.
16. Oxycodone or Oxycontin, another painkiller.
17. Adderall, a medication used in the treatment of attention deficit hyperactive disorder.

that my therapist was back in Wyoming, and I could get her a letter next week if she'd write me a prescription. She agreed that it would be dangerous for me to stop taking estrogen cold turkey, so she wrote me up a script and put me on some antiandrogens too. When I ran out of those, I went back to see her again, and she asked about my letter again. I expected her to kick me out of her office when I told her that I never had a letter to begin with.

She said, "The letter is to prove that you want to transition, and if you're willing to go this far, you're obviously not going to change your mind. I'm going to keep writing you prescriptions, but you have to promise me you'll come back and have your blood work done."

I was so grateful that I agreed to come back as often as she wanted, even if I was a little nervous about what they'd find if they tested my blood. [laughs]

Hormone replacement therapy changes one's body gradually. Initial effects can start within the first month of beginning hormonal treatment and continue throughout the next two to three years.[18]

QUINN

Most people get tired of me talking about my body hair within the first five minutes, but my girlfriend has been great about it. She will listen to me talk about how patchy my leg hair is, or how my right leg is hairier than my left leg. She'll sympathize when I complain that my butt is itchy because all of this hair is coming in. She will scratch my back for me because I have so many hairs sprouting up and it's so itchy. I don't even know how much of a shit she gives about my body hair, but she never stops listening to me talk about it.

"Can you see my moustache?"

Even though I have virtually no hair on my upper lip, she always says, "Yeah, it's huge! It's furry. It's like a caterpillar, really."

18. After several years of consistent hormone use, continued changes to secondary-sex characteristics occur but tend to be subtle.

HUGO

I was on hormones for about five months before I lost my insurance. I was also having trouble with transitioning faster than I was ready, and issues with my [increased] sex drive made it difficult for me to deal with my [previous] sexual assaults, so I got off of it for a year. I've been back on for the past six months, and it's much better this time. I'm on a lower dose now than my doctor thinks I should be, but it's what's good for me, even if it's not good on paper.

WENDY

My transition was delayed greatly by my divorce. My wife left me when I told her I wanted to be a woman, that I was a woman, and my life became a chaotic blur. Even though my marriage had ended because I wanted to transition, my transition didn't begin for two more years. It just never seemed like the right time.

By the time I started taking hormones, I was in a relationship with a fabulous woman, Betsy, whose daughter also happened to be trans. Betsy and I were engaged, and I had recently moved into their house, which was a major adjustment for everyone involved. My soon-to-be stepdaughter, Jordi, and I basically began our transitions at the same time. It was like a comedy of errors.

In some ways we could bond over how the estrogen made us feel and the new effects that we were noticing in our bodies. I feel like it helped to bring us closer. At the same time, there is a major generational gap that we've never been able to cross. I'm older than Betsy, so I'm old enough to be Jordi's grandmother. I dislike how kids are so attached to their phones and gadgets these days, and Jordi never stops texting her friends. She hates how illiterate I am with technology. Jordi gets a lot of her information about transitioning from that YouTube thing. I get my information from books and face-to-face interactions. Conversation is quickly becoming a lost art.

Betsy has graciously mediated the relationship that Jordi and I have. Since we started hormones at the same time, we both went through mood swings at the same time. Having two trans women who are both relearning how to regulate their emotions living under one roof is a lot like putting two of those betta fish in the same tank: there were days when I thought we would tear one another apart. Betsy always intervened compassionately at just the right moments.

Many trans folk liken beginning hormone replacement therapy to going through puberty. As hormonal changes take place and secondary-sex characteristics shift, some trans people experience mood swings, changes in libido, and changes in energy levels. Estrogen can cause breast budding and tenderness, typical of female puberty, while testosterone can cause acne and voice cracking, typical of male puberty.

OWEN

Testosterone affects the size and shape of your genitals. For a lot of trans guys, one of the first things they notice when they start taking T is an enlargement of their clitoris by a few centimeters.

A few months ago, I texted a nude photo of myself to my wife while she was in class. She's a really good student and she doesn't normally look at her phone until she's out of class, so I didn't think it would be a problem. Apparently it was a slow day, so she opened the message and my junk popped up on the screen.

One of her friends was in the seat next to her and glanced over at just the wrong time. She leans over to my wife and says, "Huh, his stuff doesn't look like our stuff."

Then she leaned over to another of their friends said, "Hey, check out this picture of Owen naked."

The third friend looks at it and says, "What do you know? He really does have junk!"

Upon starting testosterone, many trans men experience clitoral growth. The average enlargement is between one to three centimeters, but some experience this change to a much greater extent. Additionally, testosterone can cause changes in the pH levels of the vagina and urinary tract leading to increased urinary tract infections.

I have chronically occurring urinary tract infections [UTIs], which are really common in women and not so common in men. Every time I go to the doctor, they'll say, "Well, UTIs aren't very common in men, so we need to test you for STDs."

I know I don't have an STD. I know my body; I have a UTI. Not to mention that I'm monogamous. So, for the twentieth time, I'll explain to the offending nurse or doctor, "I'm biologically female. I have a vagina. I have a urinary tract infection."

Then they'll put me on antibiotics.

If I miss a day of work, I can't say that I have a urinary tract infection, nor can I say that I have a kidney infection, because it might raise a red flag. I have to lie and say kidney stones or something else that won't raise an eyebrow. This is such common knowledge that I've been told by nondoctors, "You have a UTI? That's so uncommon in men!"

I always think, "Well, I'm a really uncommon man; I have a vagina."

Cultural competency around transgender bodies and issues is incredibly important for physicians. While hormone replacement therapy and gender-confirmation surgeries might be considered specialized care, trans folk seek medical care beyond their transitions and must rely on primary care providers and the staff of emergency departments and urgent care clinics to have a basic knowledge of their unique needs.

Of course, medical and surgical experiences are not just for patients. The experiences of providing physicians are integral to increasing medical education around trans issues. Supriya has a unique perspective on transitioning as she is both a trans woman and a physician.

SUPRIYA

I am a physician in internal medicine, currently working in New York. I went to school at the University of Washington, and I did my residency at the Johns Hopkins Hospital.

Because I am both transgender and I see transgender patients, people always ask me what trans people are looking for in a health-care provider. I don't know that I can speak to that. It's like asking, What is a woman looking for in a provider? What is an African American looking for in any provider? What is a Muslim looking for in a provider? The answer is going to be as varied as the number of people you meet. Being a patient is different from being a physician when you're treating someone. Just because you have heart disease doesn't mean you're an expert on heart disease.

As a trans patient, and the physician taking care of trans patients, my lines cross in various ways. Some of my patients know that I'm transgender, but many do not. If I feel that it is relevant to the care that I'm providing or to my relationship with the patient, I'll disclose. Sometimes I'll see patients who are very comfortable with their genders. They'll say, "Doc, I want to go on hormones. I want to transition. I know exactly what I'm doing."

The information is out there, and so many trans patients are very well educated on the issue. Other patients struggle. They don't know how to start, they don't know where to go, and they really battle with the social aspects of transitioning. For those patients, I tend to disclose my own transgender status. I had a patient who obviously wanted to transition but was worried that no one would hire him if he transitioned. He thought that transitioning would mean giving up his chances at a decent career.

I told him, "I thought the same thing when I came out, but it's been thirteen years and I'd say my career is doing just fine."

Other doctors always assume that trans patients are complicated to treat. This could not be further from the truth. It's a new thing for me on the medical side, but it's not a lot different than providing hormone therapy to cisgender patients. You don't necessarily have to cram your brain with facts and figures about transgender patients. You do that in med school, and there's a lot to learn along the way, but after ten years I can say a lot of it becomes pretty routine and boring. I can treat blood pressure with my eyes closed. Of course, you have to know the medicine part of it, but most importantly, you have to care about the people that you are trying to treat. If you want to be a good physician, it won't matter whether you're taking care of transgender patients, gay patients, or patients from different races or religions. Doctors have to have compassion and keep it, and if they don't have it, they have to find it.

Anything That Was Going to Be This Expensive, I Was Going to Have Fun With

Some trans individuals seek surgical procedures that will bring their bodies more in line with the gender with which they identify. Surgeries can include genital reassignment; mastectomy or breast augmentation; hysterectomy, oophorectomy, or salpingectomy; facial feminization or masculinization; or other body-contouring procedures.[19]

JAIME

I talked to my partner a lot last December about wanting to transition. He identifies as a straight man, so until I came out, we were a heterosexual couple. I was told at the time that if I decided to take hormones it would be a deal breaker. Fast-forward three or four months, I had been binding my chest since December and seeing a therapist. Finally, we sat down to talk about which things might change, could change, or must change and figure out how open we both were to them. Which aspects of transition were hard boundaries, soft boundaries, or negotiable? I was surprised to find that top surgery[20] was the only thing that I would like to change that he wasn't as comfortable with. He was supportive of everything else.

I started hormones a few months ago, and I do want top surgery eventually. I'm hoping that given some time his opinion about it will change, but if everything else stays the same I'm okay with keeping

---

19. See medical glossary for more information on these procedures.
20. Surgical procedures involving the chest or breasts. In this case, Jaime is referring to a bilateral mastectomy. See glossary.

things the way they are. He's an amazing partner, and I wouldn't trade him for the world.

HUGO

It took me a while to decide to transition. I was trying to hold on to my family, trying to hold on to my job, [and] trying to hold on to my life. I bounced back and forth between transitioning and not, all the while trying to educate my primary care physician about how to care for trans patients. When I was finally on hormones, I tried to get my doctor to write me a letter for top surgery. She kept pressuring me to get a reduction instead of a full mastectomy. I looked at her and said, "If I'm not happy with the reduction, are you going to pay for me to go back and have the rest of it removed? I can't afford to have surgery twice."

CAMERON

I did not, by any means, think I was going to get top surgery this soon. If I could have had it my way, I would have done top surgery before even starting T. I adjusted my hopes, because I knew I wouldn't have a spare eight thousand dollars for a really long time, and it wasn't covered by the insurance I was on. I assumed I was going to have to get ready for the long haul of binding forever, but last summer I got into a car accident, and I was T-boned at a stop sign. My car was totaled and I got eight thousand dollars from the insurance company. I thought, "I should buy a new car with this money," but I decided I would do the irresponsible thing and get surgery instead of a car and damn the consequences. I didn't know when I was going to have that much money again. As a result, I'm pretty broke right now, but I don't really care.

Melissa Johnson is the surgeon who performed my top surgery. She and her staff are really great, but she is a typical intense plastic surgeon. She's kind of silly because every time I'm in the office with her, she does the plastic surgeon thing where she points out something else that could use some fixing. First it was my acne and then it was my eyelids. I'm always too amused to be offended.

TAYLOR

You have to live in the gender you want to be full time for a year before they'll perform sexual-reassignment surgery,[21] which was perfect because there was about a year waiting list to get in. I scheduled my surgery with a deposit using money in my savings account. It felt a lot like applying for college because you have to give a personal history, you have to have your letters of recommendation, and letters from your therapist asserting that you've been through all the therapies. It's quite involved.

The selection of your surgeon is also very much like selecting a college. There were a few criteria that I used: price (because, of course, insurance didn't pay for any of it), experience in the field, [and] trying to minimize the number of surgeries I would have to have. I finally decided to go with Marci Bowers in what was the fabulous sex-change capital of the world, Trinidad, Colorado. She herself was trans so I figured she had both inside and outside experience in this surgery and understood what it meant to trans people.

I was busy with graduating so the surgery date crept up on me. First it was the month before, then the week, [and] then two days before. The day before my surgery I drove up with my mom; it was a little road trip across New Mexico, and like always, we bought burritos at this place called "Santa Fe Grill" in Las Cruces. We took turns driving, and we were really concerned about snow over the mountain pass because it was early February, but we didn't have any problems that day.

We made it to Trinidad, a town that was essentially built around two industries: mining and sexual-reassignment surgery. It made me think, "One of these things is not like the other." You could

---

21. Now called genital-reassignment surgery or gender-confirmation surgery.

kind of feel this animosity in the town except for the fact that all the hospital patients clearly brought in money to all of the hotels and restaurants. It's this really weird place. I probably saw more trans people there than I ever had at one time, except for at transgender conferences. It was like a *Twilight Zone* episode.

I was scheduled for the first surgery in the morning. We had to be there by 5:00 a.m. It had snowed pretty heavily the night before, and being from New Mexico, we were not prepared to deal with that. My mom and I got dressed really quickly and went out to the car. We started digging the car out with plastic cups from the hotel and wiped down the windows with towels. We finally got the car out, but we didn't have four-wheel drive or snow tires so we couldn't get the car up the hill to the hospital. So, we parked and walked the last quarter of a mile in the snow until we finally arrived at the hospital.

It was when I put on my hospital gown that I started to get really nervous. I can't remember much of that day. I know it took a couple of tries to put the IV in. They took me into the operating room, and they put me on the table. The last thing I remember is the anesthesiologist talking to me about countries that I wanted to visit.

After the surgery they wheeled me into the room where my mom was waiting. Everything about the first day was just this dreamlike blur. I was so wiped out with fatigue. The second day I remember better: it hurt like a motherfucker.

ALEXANDER

I financed my top surgery through credit cards and loans. In some ways I think it was a mistake. The credit card amount just keeps going up because my car is always breaking down. On the other hand, I don't think I would be alive right now if I hadn't had surgery when I did. I wasn't suicidal, but I wasn't functional. I couldn't get out of bed. I kept hoping that I wouldn't wake up. It wasn't that I wanted to die; it was that I wanted everything to stop hurting.

Unfortunately, my surgery didn't have good results and I need a revision. One of my nipple grafts died, so my skin is just lumpy there. The other side has strange scarring that just ballooned out, so I still have to bind if I wear a tight shirt. Of course, my credit cards are maxed out, so I won't be able to afford a revision in this lifetime.

CATHERINE

I had a hilarious romp through transition because I made it that way. I was lucky that this was at the end of the nineties. If you were a registered nurse at that time, anyone would give you a credit card for twenty thousand dollars. I burned through a couple of those for my transition. I decided early on that anything that was going to be this expensive, I was going to have fun with.

The differences between the male skull and the female skull occur late in puberty. Having transitioned later in life, those differences were already set in stone. The square jaw, the sharp nose, and the protrusive eyebrow ridge are all stereotypical parts of the male skull. To "correct" those, a plastic surgeon must resect the forehead, take a centimeter off the eyebrow ridge, cut the jaw flare, and push the nose back. It took ten hours of surgery to do that to my face. Eleven years ago it cost twenty-five thousand dollars, but for me it was entirely worth it.

Before the surgery I had the forehead of a Star Trek character. I had to wear makeup and a dress in order to convince people I was a woman. Now I can wear anything I want; I can even wear men's clothes if I want to and still pass. I couldn't do that before. It's funny, because I look identical to my sister now. Relatives mistake us for one another and then they crack up when they realize what they've done.

FELIPE

I got top surgery in Seattle. It was the second time I've had top surgery, because I had a breast reduction when I was younger. At some point, I have to have a revision because I have so much scar tissue.

I can't walk around without a shirt on because of the way my scarring is. However, I can still get away with wearing just a tank top, and I *love* not wearing a binder![22]

I was very fortunate that insurance paid for my surgery. The challenge was finding someone in my provider network. Obviously, I wasn't going to find a surgeon in Alaska, so I looked at surgeons in Washington [State]. The surgeon I found hadn't really worked on trans people before, but she'd done breast reconstruction and removal, so she knew the tissue really well.

I took two and a half weeks off of work and flew down to Seattle for the surgery. After the first week, I ended up working remotely. I didn't have any vacation time, and I didn't have anyone to cover me. I told my boss something really vague to get the time off. I think I told him I had some family issues I needed to take care of down in Washington. My boss isn't the sort of guy who was going to pry. I didn't tell my coworkers anything, and I think they all thought that someone had died.

When I got back to work, I still had limited mobility. Right after I returned, there was a big bowling party, which was obviously not going to happen for me. I told my friend that I had been snowboarding and screwed up my shoulder. I went to the bowling party anyway but didn't bowl. My coworkers were trying to get me to use my left hand instead, and I think a few of them suspected something, but nobody really pushed it.

NATALIE

I had a thick, coarse beard prior to transition. I would shave in the morning, and my five o'clock shadow would start by two. I knew that before I could start my social transition, I would have to have electrolysis.

For me, it took about five hundred hours of electrolysis before my body hair was manageable. At thirty dollars an hour, this was a very expensive endeavor. In order for electrolysis to work, I had to begin

---

22. A compression shirt. See "binding" in the glossary.

taking estrogen. I started my physical transition, but I wasn't ready to disclose my identity publicly until after my hair was under control. It took about a year of going to the electrologist before I finally stopped seeing beard growth.

I Was Dysphoric the Entire Time

Dysphoria is one of the many possible consequences of delaying or withholding gender-confirming medical care from patients who wish to physically transition. Experiencing dysphoria is usually described as having a severe discomfort with one's body, or being reminded that one's body is incongruent with their desired gender. Dysphoria has many causes, and for many (but certainly not all) people who transition medically, it eases as their bodies begin to align more closely with their gender identities.

ERIK

I came out toward the end of my sophomore year of college, and everyone in my life was using my preferred name and pronouns.[23] That summer I worked for a third-party organization that contracts with the U.S. military, so I was living on a military base in Japan. I hadn't started hormones yet, and I knew things would just be easier if I tried to ignore my trans identity for a few months. The entire time I worked that job, I had to switch back to a female name and pronouns to avoid issues of violence. It was much more emotionally difficult than I thought it was going to be. I don't know what I was expecting, but I was dysphoric the entire time. It wasn't that my gender identity wasn't being respected; it was that I couldn't display it. The situation was difficult, but it was definitely a better decision than trying to be respected and safe as a trans person in a militarized space.

---

23. Usually refers to the name and pronouns that a person chooses to reflect their identity after disclosing a trans identity. Sometimes called chosen name.

I have no plans for bottom surgeries[24] unless I have a lot of money in the distant future. I would like to get a hysterectomy in the future because my period still hasn't stopped and I've been on T for seven months, so it should have stopped by now.[25] I know a few people who have been on T for three years who still menstruate, which can be very dysphoric. I hoped I wasn't going to be one of those people, but every twenty-eight days exactly . . . I've never missed a period in my entire life.

I was going through physical transition at the same time that I was working with a nonprofit organization that focuses on the needs of transgender youth. The director of the organization knows a lot about hormones and different administration methods for taking testosterone. The gold standard for taking T is to inject intramuscularly every two weeks. There are also gels and creams and patches, but they have varied results. The director told me that I could take testosterone subcutaneously, which means that I'm injecting into fat rather than muscle. I don't have to take nearly as high of a dose, and it's quite a bit less painful.

Dysphoria can not only affect a person's mental health and body image but also interfere in many aspects of their lives. Dysphoria is often particularly hindering to one's sex life.

JAIME

Kink[26] has actually been extremely helpful to me. I was having dysphoria, and there were things that had to be removed from the bedroom all of a sudden. Female-gendered language had to be removed or I was going to avoid sex. My partner was great about say-

---

24. A term for surgeries to reconstruct the genitals, typically used by trans men. See "genital-reassignment surgery" in the glossary.

25. For many trans men, menstruation ceases in the first two to six months of taking testosterone.

26. Alternative ("kinky") sexual behavior or community space.

ing, "I don't want you to feel that way or to have that reaction; let's try something else instead. How can we do this in a way that will be less dysphoric for you?"

Trying to rewrite my sex life in a typical bedroom situation felt awkward; it was easier to do things in ways that I perceived as an activity of gay men. That is, I identified as male, and my partner was male, so that would make us two gay men. I felt that the way we had sex should correspond to that. However, that concept really pushed a lot of my partner's buttons and challenged how he sexually identifies. He identifies as straight, so how could he have gay sex?

We had to renegotiate how we had sex so that I wasn't dysphoric and he wasn't uncomfortable. We role-play all the time, so I asked him, "How would you feel about engaging in these types of sexual activities in the context of a scene?"

This has allowed us to try on identities and figure out what works best for both of us. We can be who we want to be in that context. That makes me so happy because I was really concerned about how I was going to maintain a relationship with someone who identifies as a straight man, when I'm looking, sounding, and becoming more and more of a man myself.

DIANE

When you're trans it can be hard to figure out where genital dysphoria ends and asexuality[27] begins. I am one of the first in my friend group to have genital-reassignment surgery. They all want to know whether or not I will still be asexual after the surgery, when the factor of genital dysphoria is gone.

They ask me with such excitement, "Are you going to suddenly become sexual after the surgery?"

Well, I don't really know. I've lived forty-five years without being sexual, so it won't be a disappointment to me if I'm not suddenly sexual after surgery.

---

27. Asexuality, in general, is defined as the lack of a sexuality, that is, asexual people often do not experience sexual attraction. See glossary and chapter 4.

HUGO

My partner is also trans. He has had top surgery and is on hormones. He also wants bottom surgeries (to be later defined). I know it's something that is really important to him, but surgery is so damn expensive. We need a car that runs, and we want a house. I want him to be happy in his body, but every time we talk about surgery he feels selfish; he doesn't want to put off the things *we* need for the things *he* needs.

My dysphoria got so much better after my surgery. Before surgery, I couldn't orgasm, I couldn't have sex, and I didn't feel comfortable showering. I'm happy in my body now. Since [his] surgery, my partner's dysphoria has gotten worse. I think because he views himself so much as male now that those times when he's reminded that he's female are so much harder. Every time he goes to the bathroom, showers, or has sex, he is reminded that he's not fully male.

TAYLOR

I'm not particularly skilled with a lot of femininity. I have a more masculine bone structure, so femininity doesn't really cater to my body type anyway. There's a paradox where if I wear something really feminine and I look in the mirror, I feel like I'm accentuating or drawing attention to my masculine traits. That's how I feel with a lot of feminine attire: it emphasizes masculinity in a way that it's not supposed to.

My dysphoria has gotten better postsurgery. I still have some dysphoric days, but they are nowhere near as bad or as frequent as they used to be. My dysphoria used to be focused on my genitalia but has now primarily shifted to areas like my face, shoulder width, rib cage, or height. Whenever I'm dysphoric, I get mopey, and then I try to take my mind off of it. Like most trans folk, I have a grab bag of distractions that I turn to, and they make me feel better.

While dysphoria is common for many trans folk, not everyone has dysphoria. Some individuals are comfortable with their bodies regardless of whether they feel their gender identity and body align.

OWEN

I married a woman who has two kids. Her son is six, and her daughter is three now. Both of her children think of me as their father, since I've been a constant presence in their lives for the past two years.

I haven't figured out how to pay for top surgery yet, and someday I would like to, but for now I'm comfortable with my body. It's not uncommon for me to walk around the house without a shirt on. It's my house; I can be naked if I want. This isn't a problem at all, but it had led our son to think that all men have boobs. Mom has boobs, and Dad has boobs, and we're the only adults that he's seen without shirts, so in his mind all adults have boobs. The other day he told me that he's really excited to grow up so that he can have boobs too!

RUSS

I have a lot of fears about transitioning. I can't guarantee that my family would support me. Plus, I can't afford it. I've spent the past year playing with my gender, trying on new identities. Last school year I used male pronouns and explored a very masculine identity, which helped me to figure out that I don't want to be forced to give up my lesbian identity by becoming male.

I think one of the reasons I'm not pressing a hormonal intervention is because I'm so comfortable with my body. I can look at myself naked and not have a problem with it. For me, that confidence really relates to sports. I'm an athlete, so I'm not only in tune with my body [but] also comfortable showering and changing in the locker room. At this point I don't know if I have more of a preference for feminine or masculine pronouns, so I typically go by gender neutral.[28] I may still transition someday, but I don't want to rush into anything unless I'm absolutely sure. I'm pretty laid back about it.

---

28. Sets of pronouns that deviate from he/him/his and she/her/hers.

Transitioning on the Job

Beyond disclosing a trans identity to friends and family, trans individuals often have to negotiate their transition in the workplace. Some employers are supportive, but there are still a number of states in which a person can be fired on the basis of their gender identity or expression. This means when a person transitions on the job, or discloses a trans status to their employer, they can be let go. To avoid the potentiality of being fired, some trans folk elect[29] to quit their jobs on good terms prior to transitioning.

CAMERON

I worked for a while at a local fish market. I quit when I got top surgery. I was considering going back to work after my surgery, but my coworkers were a strange mix of wary and supportive. Some of my coworkers knew I was trans and they told some other people, and word just spread. Eventually, the owner of the market started using masculine pronouns for me, even though I hadn't told him I was trans. It was a mix of good and awkward, but for my sanity I decided not to return to work after surgery.

QUINN

When I went back to school in the fall, I was debating whether I should come out slowly and ease myself into transition a few months into the semester or come out prior to the beginning of the term. I decided it would be way easier if on day one I said, "Everyone, this is my name, these are my pronouns."

NATALIE

I wore women's clothing at home, and my family had started using my preferred name and pronouns, but as soon as I left the house I had to be a man again. I was so excited to finally get to start

---

29. Here "elect" is not really the choice it implies. Some trans folk "choose" the lesser of two evils by quitting their jobs to avoid the risk of physical or emotional harassment.

being myself full time. When my beard was virtually gone, I started taking a higher dose of estrogen, which led to more and more physical changes. I knew I was running out of time to come out at work. Transitioning on the job is not an easy thing to do but even less so when you're a police officer in a small town. There was only so long I could manage to avoid the locker room, and if I went in, someone would be bound to notice a few things.

I asked the police chief if we could have a word. He's a nice guy, but that didn't mean he was going to be supportive of my transition. Before I came out to him, I had started applying for other jobs. I was certain he was going to fire me. I sat him down and told him that I had started taking estrogen and that I'd had electrolysis. I told him that I was going to need a few weeks off for surgery and that it was his choice whether or not I returned to work after. I just figured that if he wasn't going to be supportive, it wasn't a place where I wanted to work. I gave him the opportunity to make that decision.

Much to my amazement he said, "You know, I've got an aunt who used to be my uncle. I don't give a shit if you're a man or a woman. As long as you do your damn job, it doesn't matter to me which uniform you wear. Do you want to tell the others yourself, or do you want me to do it?"

I indicated that it might be easier if he called a meeting to explain the situation. He said, "Don't worry about it. If anyone gives you any grief, you just have them take it up with me."

I was in a euphoric daze as I stood up. I thanked him over and over again, and I had just reached the door of his office when he called out, "What's you're name going to be?"

I told him that I was going to change it to Natalie after surgery. He nodded and said, "Great. I'll order you a new badge."

I broke into tears the second I left the station.

ERIK

I was working in a retail store, and it was case by case which customers would read me as male. I had short hair and wore the men's uniform, so little kids and older people would perceive me as male. My voice hadn't changed yet, but my nametag said Erik. People asked me all the time, "Are you a boy or girl?"

When I was read as female, no one saw me as effeminate. I was a very masculine woman, but as soon as people started reading me as male, they would see me as feminine. To them, I was a fairy. I was a faggot. When I started taking T, my voice dropped. People started seeing me as male, but somehow, they didn't view me as masculine anymore. This made me very uncomfortable, and I struggled with my own internalized homophobia for a long time.

I also struggled with the loss of my dyke identity. I have two lesbian coworkers in my office right now. They view me as peripheral family,[30] because they think I'm a gay boy. However, they don't see me as a dyke, and I don't have the same connection with them that I might otherwise. There aren't a lot of queer spaces where I feel accepted, especially since I lost all of the lesbian ones. That was the hardest part of transition for me. I'm much, much more comfortable identifying as faggy or fairy now, but it took a very long time.

Transition can thrust trans folk (and their partners or polys[31]) into new categories of sexual identity. Some, like Erik, grieve the loss of their former sexual identity. Couples might likewise feel displaced when one partner transitions. Learning to navigate within a new sexuality community can be a difficult undertaking.

LUIS

I auditioned for a traveling theater troupe, and much to my surprise I was cast as male. One of the plays we're doing is a musical. I'm taking a very low dose of T, and my voice is slowly changing, but I'm not quite sure how that's going to affect my singing. I haven't disclosed my trans status to the troupe yet. I think I'm going to try

---

30. *Family* is a term sometimes used by LGBTQI people to indicate other LGBTQI people.
31. Member of a polyamorous relationship. See "polyamory" in the glossary.

and feel out the vibe of the troupe before I say anything. Most of the other actors and actresses are pretty much hippies, so I'm hoping they will be accepting. I'd be surprised if they weren't; in general, theater is a very gay space.

CATHERINE

I was a school nurse at Proctor Academy for ten years, and that's where I transitioned. My therapist challenged me. "Why do you have to leave? Give it a shot."

I sat down with various administrators before the start of the term and told them that I was going to transition and that I wanted to keep my job. They asked what my transition would look like. I told them that not a lot would change, except that I would start coming to work in dresses. I was always effeminate. I already wore multiple earrings. My nails were always painted. If anything, I looked more natural in a dress than I did in men's clothing. Once they came to this realization, all of the administrators were very supportive of me.

FELIPE

I am a project-controls professional for a construction management company in Alaska. I help plan and manage the costs on construction and engineering projects. When I worked in the Anchorage office, most of the administrative assistants were women, and most of the managerial staff were men. Amongst the engineers, there was a pretty even split between men and women. I now work on the northern slope of Alaska, which is the very northern edge. It takes an hour-and-a-half plane ride from Anchorage to get here. When you work up here, you stay in dorm-style housing. There are only three women in our group of twenty.

If I weren't stealth, it wouldn't hinder my career greatly. Emotionally and mentally, it would be suicide. I knew I would have to be stealth when I accepted a job in Alaska. Living in the dorms adds to that necessity. I have to think a little bit more about the way in which

I'm conveying my gender, but after a few years it's just starting to become part of my routine.

Being Nonbinary in a Binary World

Much of the dominant culture of the United States is divided into a binary separation of men and women. From bathrooms to clothing departments and toy aisles to careers, we are constantly inundated with messages about how to conform to preconceived notions of masculinity or femininity. When people do not identify as strictly male or strictly female, it can be difficult to navigate socially.

ERIK

There are so many elements to gender that most people never stop to think about. Trans people think about these things constantly. After I came out as trans, I realized I was going to need to update my wardrobe. I gave my cute little skirts and frilly shirts to my sister and slowly began replacing everything in my closet with men's clothes. Some of the items I had I was able to hang on to, but it's amazing how gendered clothing really is. I'd take out each article and examine it. Can I keep this shirt? No, it has darts. Can I keep this one? Yes, it doesn't have capped sleeves.

After weeding through my closets and having very little left to wear, I had to start shopping for more masculine attire. As a very tall person, I actually have an easier time finding men's clothes that fit than I did women's clothes. That's lucky for me. I have a transmasculine friend who is four eleven, and he has to shop in the little boy's section in order to find anything that will fit him. When I was first starting out, I didn't know what my size was in men's clothing because the way we come up with clothing sizes is very different for men and women. I would grab a bunch of shirts that I hoped would fit and head for the dressing room.

Before I started testosterone, I could use the men's changing room as long as I didn't speak. If I was in a place with a dressing-room attendant, and they asked me how many pieces of clothing I was taking in with me, I would hold up my fingers. I knew that if I spoke, they would point me toward the women's dressing room. I know some rudimentary American Sign Language so I feigned deafness a lot during that period of transition.

MOSLEY

I don't know why clothes are gendered anyway—men's shirt, women's shirt—if it fits you well, wear the damn shirt.

TAYLOR

I spend so much time in my head thinking about dress as an extension of self and how people build community or identity based around dress. A lot of trans women, though certainly not all, try to emphasize their femininity early in transition. Society tells us that any scrap of masculinity that can be observed is a threat to your feminine identification, so there is a pressure to exhibit more feminine modes of dress. Even though I transitioned long ago, I do still feel that pressure to conform in a very effeminate fashion.

For the most part, I have established myself as more of a tomboy. When I do dress in a more feminine way, I get much more social recognition in terms of positive reinforcement. I always get compliments when I wear a skirt, so I see it as praise for what society considers correct, feminine behavior.

While some transgender individuals transition neatly from male identities or expressions to female identities or expressions or vice versa, there are many others who do not feel that they fit into such binary categories as male or female and prefer to express their genders outside of a masculine/male, feminine/female dichotomy.

SETH

In 2001, I started an all-genders, all-ages support group in the San Francisco Bay Area. At the time, there really was no other group like ours. There was FTM International for FTMs [female to males] who were transitioning along a predefined path; there was an MTF [male to female] group along the same lines, with hierarchies around who had transitioned more; and there was a youth-specific group at Lyric, but you had to be under twenty-four or twenty-five to attend. I was just outside that age. It was really important to me to cross all of these identities, so I created United Genders of the Universe. I wanted to bring people together, create support, and talk about things in a confidential space that were difficult to talk about.

At that time, the word genderqueer had just made its appearance. It didn't yet have a definition that anyone could point to. For the purposes of the group, I defined it on the fliers I gave out: anyone who views gender as having more than two options. Being genderqueer was about a mindset, as opposed to a state of transition or a certain type of gender expression.

I made sure our group was really antihierarchy. I was against the idea that some people were more "in" or more desirable than others. I wanted to have anyone who wanted to be there to be there, so long as they could respect where other people were coming from in terms of their identities. There was both a support and a discussion component in the group. We addressed major questions. How do we come out to our families? How do we go about getting jobs? How do we deal with it when people don't want us around their kids? How do we answer when people ask if we're a boy or a girl?

We made bumper stickers that addressed the struggles of being nonbinary in a binary world. They said, "Are you a boy or a girl? No. Are you?"

DAKOTA

I was nineteen when I came to the University of Vermont for school, and it was around that time that I began to figure out my agender[32] identity. I'm a sort of subset of genderqueer, in that I feel

---

32. An identity that describes a feeling or state of being genderless. See glossary.

like I don't really have a gender at all. I don't feel male or female: I have elements of both sexes, or maybe neither.

As a student, I became somewhat involved in the campus queer community. I knew I was bisexual at the time, and I decided that I wanted to be an ally to the trans community. I didn't really know anything about trans communities, so I started to research and I realized that transitioning sounded like a good fit for me. It is sometimes tricky to explain this to people because the word *transition* has become coopted by the trans community to mean a very specific process that begins with hormones and ends with surgery, but that doesn't really apply to me. My transition is an affirmation of my agender identity—not a sex change.

I'm transitioning in a way that isn't necessarily the norm. I haven't taken any hormones because a lot of the effects that I wanted from testosterone are things that require you to stay on it your whole life. Many of the early effects, like acne and body hair, were not things that I wanted and are irreversible. Taking hormones might be the right answer for me down the road, but it's not right now.

Since I'm not taking hormones, I am in speech therapy to try to lower my voice. I had a hysterectomy last year, and I'm having top surgery later this year. I was careful about the surgeons I chose. I did some extensive research to figure out who had what requirements, since many surgeons won't perform gender-affirming surgeries unless you've taken hormones. Fortunately, all of the medical professionals in the area have been really good about respecting my identity.

JAIME

There are so many queer people who hate labeling themselves. I enjoy labels because I can mash them all together. I like cutting up the boxes and creating pretty pictures with them, finding as many words as I can to describe different parts of me. I identify as genderqueer because I don't feel that I'm a guy or a girl. At the same time, I don't feel comfortable presenting as feminine, so I'm somewhat transmasculine.

I figured out about a year ago that there were terms for people who weren't one sex or the other, that there were a whole host of nonbinary terms. I began to think that maybe not everyone had to work as hard as I did to keep up the act of trying to fit in to their genders. I met a few trans boys who were genderqueer, and I both liked them and wanted to be them. It was the first time I really realized that there was something other than bisexuality happening within my life.

I'm on a really low dose of transdermal testosterone, and I might have top surgery someday, but I'm primarily read as androgynous. It has been difficult navigating queer spaces as someone with a nonbinary identity. The queer community really likes their boxes. Even a lot of mainstream transgender communities are unwelcoming to nonbinary people. They exhibit the same type of attitude you get from a lot of mainstream gay and lesbian communities: "Oh, you're bisexual? Get off the fence and decide!"

They fail to understand that androgyny, just like bisexuality, is really a place.

LACY

I exist in this unrecognized space where I'm not transgender or cisgender. I identify as fae. I'm male and I don't have any intention of taking estrogen, but I've had breast implants and I have a more effeminate body. Being fae is really about owning my own femininity. I'm certainly not a high femme,[33] but I like to express my femininity with a little more flair.

It was a process to figure out exactly how I wanted to express my gender. There aren't a lot of options for people who don't want to transition all the way. People will tell me that I'm not a woman because I have a penis, or that I must be a woman because I have breasts. I don't really care what they say; I know I have the best of both worlds!

---

33. An extremely feminine gender expression. See glossary.

DAKOTA

It's really challenging to maintain a nonbinary identity. I have an androgynous name and appearance, but people falter with regards to pronouns. In my work environment a lot of people really want to be inclusive, but there aren't really any standard gender-neutral pronouns, so I usually tell people to use whatever feels comfortable for them. I have friends who consistently switch back and forth, and others who try to avoid pronouns altogether. Our language doesn't offer a whole lot of options, and it's so heavily gendered in a lot of ways. People want to know what to do to be respectful, but there's not a lot of concrete instruction I can give them. A lot of people at work still default to calling me "she," but in public I get called "sir" a lot. My friends ask if it bothers me when people assume my pronouns, and I always tell them, of course not.

There is not a right answer, so by default there is no wrong answer.

You Can't Do It Alone

Having a sense of community is often incredibly important to well-being. An overwhelming percentage of trans folk experience inordinate amounts of trauma and oppression in their daily lives, so finding sites of support is imperative.

MOSLEY

We literally put on all of these different labels in the same way that we try on clothes. It really has a lot to do with having a solid sense of self and a foundational sense of being healthy. We get so much shit from everywhere: whether it be from family, from friends, or from society at large. We experience really oppressive trauma, and it's really good to have a place for respite and to see people who look like you who are going through the same struggles as you.

You Really Have to Appeal to Certain Expectations

Often, trans individuals find community and support in LGBTQI spaces. Historically, trans folk have been a critical force in the struggle for gay, lesbian, and bisexual rights.

JUANITA

I haven't talked to my parents since my dad found out I was gay. I've talked to my sister, who is supportive, and she always passes on my phone number in case my parents decide to talk to me, but they've never called.

When I arrived in San Francisco, I didn't have a place to stay. I didn't have a job and had very little money left over after buying my bus ticket. The first thing I did was take the BART to the Castro, that magical neighborhood I had heard so much about. It was nighttime when I got there, and I was so tired from the bus ride that I just plopped down on a bench and went to sleep. The next morning, I woke up to that big, beautiful rainbow flag flapping overhead, and I knew I was home.

QUINN

After I graduated, I moved to Manhattan for the summer, and I found a support group for transmasculine people at an LGBT center. I was like, "Hell, yeah!"

I cried the entire first session and the entire hour train ride home, because I had no idea what was happening, I just knew it was something good. I went back to the group throughout the summer because I realized that those were my people. It finally felt good. The people in the group were great. They were so respectful of the struggles I was going through and seemed to actually care about me, and were worried about me. People I didn't know would come up to me to check in on me. I ended up making all of these new friends who were very affirming of all of these different parts of my identity.

DAKOTA

My identity isn't the same as many of my trans friends' identities. We've all figured out who we are and who we want to be in our own ways. Some of us take hormones, some have surgeries, some do one but not the other, and some do nothing medical at all. Identity politics can be so divisive for communities, but I feel that sharing a common dysphoric experience is more connecting than what we decide to do about that experience.

BELLA

My boss at work is same-gender loving,[1] and it's been great to have someone who I know will go to bat for me if the need arises. I came out to her last spring, and she's been amazingly supportive. She's said, "I know you aren't out at work and that's cool, but if that ever happens to change, let me know and I'll be in your corner."

I legally changed my name this summer, and she said to let her know if anyone gives me problems about it.

RUSS

I have a trans friend who is very conservative. We went to the same undergraduate college, and our relationship has gotten better since I've moved. We don't agree on anything. Politically, we're always at odds.

Not living in the same town anymore has actually been really beneficial to our friendship. We can have very interesting discussions online, over Facebook, or through online chat. We don't agree, but we enjoy arguing with one another in a purely academic way. Our friendship has been strengthened by distance.

The last time I saw her, we went to a coffee shop together to hang out, and the conversation was very much forced. We don't have anything in common, so we don't have anything to talk about. We have a harder time arguing with one another in person because we know that could lead to a very socially awkward situation, so we're much more reserved around one another. If we do argue, we don't have the hours we need to think up a suitable reply as we would online. But she's family,[2] so even if the conversation is forced, we maintain a friendship and I make an effort to see her whenever we're in close proximity.

---

1. Another term for gay/lesbian or homosexual, often used in communities of color.
2. In this case, family is used as term for someone who is a recognized member of an LGBTQI community, not a legal or biological relative.

CATHERINE

Even before I transitioned, I had been a part of the queer women's community. No one was quite sure how I ended up there, but it's definitely where I fit. When I was first transitioning, I wore a lot of dresses and fingernail polish and makeup. My dyke friends were like, "Just stop. Please, will you stop?"

It seemed unnatural to this particular group of women that I would want to wear the sort of clothes they despised. When I asked why she was so opposed to my dress, my friend Bonnie said, "I hate wearing dresses because I was forced to."

I replied, "But I was forbidden to."

Her eyes went wide as comprehension dawned on her face. These days, Bonnie wears dresses more than she ever did, partly because now it is her choice and partly because it's not a political statement anymore.

When trans people ask how we, as trans folk, are a part of this LGBT movement, it always confounds me. We've always been here. This is us. Even though individual people say stupid things, this is our family. This is what we have.

The community has changed so much. When I transitioned, I didn't go into the bathroom at a women's bar, a gay bar, without someone at my back. Bad shit was going to happen if I did. A lot of dykes in that generation were not always welcoming to trans women, but we stuck it out and we're welcome more often than not now.

I feel like there are fewer people in the LGBT community who are purposefully exclusionary in this day and age, but it only takes a few assholes to ruin it for everyone. I think it's for this reason that there are so many people in our community who transition out of the community. You don't know it, because so many people are in early or mid-transition, but all they want to do is get through it, so they can disappear. It's only been in the last ten years or so that statistics have started keeping track of trans men. It is so easy to go stealth. You can take hormones and just pass, which is a huge privilege. I wish I had a little more than contempt for those people, but I don't.

LGBTQI communities are extremely heterogeneous. Communities consisting of people from a wide array of socioeconomic statuses, races, ethnicities, political backgrounds, national origins, and abilities often have difficulty finding enough common ground upon which to build lasting relationships. LGBTQI communities are frequently split over differing ideologies about the acceptance of nonnormative gender identities, including trans and genderqueer folks. Some lesbian, gay, and bisexual individuals believe that advocating for transgender, genderqueer, and intersex[3] issues will detract from mainstream issues, while others unknowingly create unwelcoming environments through a lack of inclusion or representation.

HUGO

I grew up a few miles away from Provincetown, Massachusetts, which is sort of a gay mecca, but I only saw lesbians, men, and drag queens. When I was a kid, I thought I was a transvestite but backward. Transvestites are frequently made fun of, so I never talked about these feelings to anyone growing up.

I knew I was different, but I didn't feel like the word "lesbian" was a good fit for me. I went up to a girlfriend of mine one day and said, "You're more gay than straight, but you're more male than female." It was a strange thing to say, but I didn't have any vocabulary. She told me to go to this youth center where I met all of these people who were trans. I was out of the closet that day to myself and to everyone there. It wasn't until about a year later that I came out to my family.

I delayed coming out because people in Provincetown are sur-

---

3. Term for a person born with atypical chromosomal, hormonal or genital configurations. See glossary.

prisingly unaccepting of transgender individuals. Being gay and lesbian is permissible and celebrated, but there isn't much in the way of trans visibility in Provincetown. The community is ridiculously liberal on issues of feminism and gay rights but fairly conservative about gender.

WENDY

I felt really invalidated every time I went into the queer community. It was so much worse to have people refuse to use my preferred pronouns or to continually gender me in a way I told them I wasn't comfortable with. It's offensive in my own space, but it's even more offensive when it comes from someone in the queer community who should know better. I've had to try to find support systems at an individual level, which has been challenging.

MOSLEY

I've lived in really large urban areas such as Atlanta and New Orleans where there is not only a solid, intact queer community but also a solid, intact, active queer community of color. This is incredibly important and valuable to me. A lot of things that are community specific to being part of a community of color don't necessarily translate to the ways that people represent the queer community.

For those of us who are masculine of center,[4] you see our identities in our dress, style, and walk. We also identify as black, as Latino, or as Native. We identify across the board, yet our experiences aren't reflected in LGBTQ conversations. When there is talk about LGBTQ issues, often issues of gay, privileged white men take center stage. The arguments become about marriage equality — and don't get me wrong I'm very supportive of marriage equality; I want my rights, dammit — but issues of homelessness, sexual violence, racial discrimination, and housing discrimination are completely ignored. These are all more pressing issues than wanting your partner to get

---

4. A term for masculine women, used primarily in communities of color.

the same benefits that you have at your really elite job. Many people in poor communities or communities of color can't even talk about benefits right now, because we're not getting work. We're not safe in our communities, and often we're not safe from the very institutions that are supposed to protect us: law enforcement, social services, and other institutions that are supposed to help our community [but] have often marginalized us in many ways.

CAMERON

I went to Mount Holyoke College in Massachusetts, which is a women's college. I have really mixed feelings about my time there. When I was in high school, I was really avid about going to Mount Holyoke. I visited the campus, and I really liked the idea of going to a women's college. It also had the added bonus that my parents didn't really want me to go there. [laughs] They told me, "You need to go where you are exposed to both sexes, you can't just cut out half the world."

They even had a friend, who was an alum of Mount Holyoke, warn me about the radical lesbian community there. I ended up going anyways, but I never really quite felt like I fit in.

My freshman year I came out as a lesbian, and I was really at odds with the gay community on campus a lot of the time. I didn't like how the cool kids on campus were in the gay clique and that animosity snowballed into other areas of my life as my gender identity became more and more fluid. By the end, I wanted to run out of there as fast as I could. I don't know if I would have transitioned sooner or not had I gone to a coed school. Part of the Mount Holyoke environment kept me in the mindset that I was the worst lesbian in the world. At the same time, there is a much more lax attitude toward cross-dressing and appearing more butch[5] than there might be at a similar-sized liberal arts school.

---

5. Often a masculine-presenting lesbian. See glossary.

OLIVIA

I came out later in life, and I am therefore ignorant to many of the politics that govern the LGBT community. One of the interesting things I've noticed is how different parts of this group celebrate. Lesbian, gay, bisexual, and other people whose identities are based on sexuality celebrate at pride parades and similar events. These holidays are about being open and out, and about celebrating their beauty and their spirit. Pride is an opportunity for LGB people to be out in public and let everyone know that they are not ashamed of themselves.

There are trans people who participate in pride, but for the most part, trans folk are forced to be spectacles every day so they aren't necessarily interested in throwing a parade where even more people can gawk at them. The biggest celebration in the transgender community is Trans Day of Remembrance, where we hold vigils to memorialize our dead. The rates of suicide, murder, and drug overdose in the trans community are astronomically high. People in all parts of the world gather each November with pictures of our trans loved ones. We celebrate their lives and mourn their deaths.

We're still too plagued by death to be able to celebrate pride. Trans folk participating in pride events could very well leave them open and vulnerable to harassment. We don't have basic rights and basic safeties, so no, we're not really interested in helping you plan your pride parade. This is what the LGB side of the community doesn't understand.

RAFAEL

Studs and aggressives[6] don't have much of an obvious presence in the world. Most mainstream media, film, and academic literature are very much whitewashed. We're looking for ways to fill that breadth and also to communicate across difference. It's difficult

---

6. Often terms for masculine women, typically used by people of color. See glossary.

when there are so few depictions of queerness in which we can see ourselves reflected. That's a conversation we've been having in the black community for a long time, because we have very limited representation as well. Is it better for us to have a black person in a movie, so we can have at least one black movie a year, or do the depictions of that movie matter? I think queer folks and people of color are in a similar space. Should we be invisible and not have a space, or should we have a space that is totally problematic, incomplete, and one dimensional?

GREG

Queer communities often use the word *family* to mean chosen family. These are our best friends and lovers and role models and mentees. We build very intricate, multigenerational family structures comprised entirely of queer folks. This helps us navigate a landscape where either our biological families have rejected us or our partners and children are not legally recognized as our families due to discriminatory laws and policies.

I have some friends who I'm only friends with because we're queer. In high school it was very much about being a part of the community. It has become really hard to maintain some of those relationships, because we have nothing else in common. There are a handful of people who I don't even like as a human being or as a person, but they're queer so I feel the "family" connection. It's getting harder and harder to want to maintain these meaningless relationships.

TAYLOR

To survive in the mainstream LGBT community, you really have to appeal to certain expectations. This community seems to be really enamored with transmasculinity and genderqueer identity, and there's not really a place in either of those two categories for a good chunk of trans women. If we can't fit in with the queer community, where do we fit?

They're My Biggest Fans

Looking outside of LGBTQI communities for support, many trans folk have turned to families and partners, or have created social support networks based on common interests.

FELIPE

My family wasn't originally supportive of my transition, but it's amazing how making six figures makes your family all suddenly love you. In all seriousness, getting a job that used my education and that paid in the range that it should for a graduate with my degree really turned their opinions around. My dad was afraid that I was going to screw myself out of a future by transitioning. Showing them that I can still get a good job with a good company really put a lot of their fears at bay. It showed them that transitioning wasn't going to ruin my life.

I've spent more time with my family in the last ten months than I had in the previous seven years. I've been trying to get to Seattle more often, because my grandparents from Costa Rica just moved up there. My grandfather is ninety years old, so I'm trying to get in as much time as I can with him. I went down for my sister's graduation, I went down for my cousin's wedding, and I went down for Thanksgiving. All of a sudden, my family has reentered my life, and they are a really important support for me.

OWEN

My parents and siblings don't speak to me anymore. I have one aunt who still sends me a Christmas card, but everyone else has basically abandoned me. It used to really bother me, but now that I'm an adult and I have my own family it doesn't seem as big of a deal. I spend all of my time outside of work with my wife and kids, and they're my biggest fans. They are always there for me even if they don't know exactly how it is that they're supporting me.

We haven't told our kids that I'm transgender yet, because they just aren't old enough to be trusted to not repeat that information. We've introduced the concept to them in age-appropriate terms, but we're not ready to fully disclose my trans status. Our three-year-old is at a stage where she repeats everything she hears with very little concept of what it means. If we told her I was trans, I can just see her sitting in the cart at the grocery store telling every stranger that passes, "My daddy used to be a girl! My daddy has a vagina!"

WILSON

My mom is really supportive. There are lots of kids who get kicked out of their houses, but my mom has been really cool about everything. She works as a nurse, so she knows a lot about the medical stuff, and being trans wasn't anything new to her. My brother has been pretty cool about everything too. For my birthday he took me out to buy a tie and some men's dress shoes. I'm not on testosterone yet, but once I am he said he'd help me pick out a razor and teach me how to shave.

MIRIAM

The first time I ever came across any mention of trans people was in a book at Hebrew school. I think it was called *Yifat, Who Wishes She Wasn't a Girl*. The book never explicitly states that the character is trans, but the concept of gender transgression is undeniable. I read this book over and over again, and when I asked my parents about it, they basically told me, "Sometimes boys want to become girls, and sometimes girls want to be boys."

They didn't elaborate or convey any judgment either way. It was enough to let me know that other people had the same feelings as me, and that knowledge was enough to sustain me for years.

Instead of relying on families to provide support, sometimes interest-based communities can provide networks of inclusion and encouragement.

JAIME

As an overall culture, geek culture[7] has been the most accepting of my transition, much more so than the queer community. They'll say, "Oh you're going to cosplay[8] as a girl in a dress? Cool. The guy with the kilt and the long hair wants to be called Nancy? We don't care. As long as you've got your dice, we're good to go."

Geeks tend to care the least about gender and stereotypes. Most of the geeks I know are also kinky, and the kinky ones are usually also polyamorous.[9] It's a wonderful little trifecta of people who support one another, whatever they do.

TAYLOR

I'm not particularly interested in hanging out with people just because they are gay or queer or trans; it's such a boring root of community. I've met so many trans people, and I've got nothing to talk to them about except for the assumed shared experience of being trans. I prefer to hang out with nerds who are watching Dr. Who and who have read John Green's books. I have found nerd communities feel a lot more accepting than many GLBT communities; I could go hang out in online nerd forums and talk about gender or being trans, which is a conversation that a lot of gay folks aren't willing to have.

In middle school one of my best friends was named Maya. Maya was really into the Sailor Moon cartoons, and she would talk about it all the time. I decided I should figure out what it was all about, so I went home and I started watching the show. I ended up really liking it. When I watch a show that I really like, I'll start identifying more

---

7. While some of the individuals I interviewed found "geek culture" to be a welcoming space, others commented that geek spaces are frequently not welcoming to people of color.

8. Short for costume play, cosplay involves role-playing a character while wearing costumes. See cosplay and crossplay in glossary.

9. Polyamory usually refers to having emotional, romantic, or sexual relationships with more than one partner.

with one particular character, and I tend to get a little fanatic about it. For me, that character was Sailor Venus. I have no clue why I was drawn to her so much. My friends said I was much more like Mercury, because she's the super brainy one, but Venus was the more feminine one of the whole group. This really made me start questioning my gender.

Another fictional area that made me examine my gender was the *Harry Potter* series. I imagined using magic to get myself out of various situations, and I was especially enamored with the idea of Polyjuice Potion, which is a tonic that allows the drinker to transform into another person. I wanted to take the potion and magically transform into a girl. Besides, I feel like Hogwarts is such an inclusive community. It would probably be more problematic to be muggle-born there than to be trans.

Through imagining myself in the contexts of these characters in these fantasy worlds, I started to explore my identity a lot more. I guess I've always been attracted to nerdy outlets for gender. I see people doing this same type of self-exploration with cosplay. I think people cosplay because it's fun and you actually get to *be* the character. That was something that I desperately wanted in middle school. I would have loved to have been these characters. As an adult, I frequent conventions where I can cosplay or crossplay, and I get to embody some of the characters that were really formative for me in my youth.

The role that partners play in supporting transgender individuals can be incredibly important.

CAMERON

Prior to moving to Maine, I was living in Driggs, Idaho. I graduated from college in May 2011, got in my car, and drove out to Idaho for a newspaper internship. The job was great, but I was having a hard time managing emotionally out there. I didn't know anyone, and it was just very western and sparse, and I had a hard time making friends. At the end of the internship, I packed up and drove back east. I thought, where is a place relatively close to family, with a diverse community? Portland, Maine, ended up being that place.

My partner, Grey, is a musician and an artist. He has a twenty-piece, queer and ally gypsy-folk-punk band,[10] and there are a few trans members in the band that he tours around the country with. He is also part of this poetry group in Portland that does a lot of awareness in queer communities, and I met him at a poetry workshop. I very much pursued him after that. He was a little nervous and had never been with a trans guy before. He identifies as gay. I was never stealth with him, so I never had to disclose, which was fortunate. I wasn't getting a lot of signal back, but finally he sent me a text message that said, "I think I really like you, but I've never been attracted to someone transitioning before," blah, blah, blah.

We talked about it, and I told him I identify as a man and I identify as gay. If you like me you're a gay man, end of story. He thought that these were reasonable terms, so we started dating, and he's been incredibly supportive of me.

FELIPE

I'm out to my friend Ben, my roommate, and one other trans guy. I met my roommate at a gay bar, so I knew it would be pretty safe to come out to her. I figured out early on that I needed at least one person to ground me. It was really important to me to be able to tell her. That way, I have someone to talk to in person if I need to. I also have one coworker in her midforties who knows. I told her after about a year of working there.

Being stealth is something that you get used to after a while. However, dating gets really tiring. I don't feel any need anymore to tell my friends. I know very little about their childhoods, so I don't have any desire to over-share about mine. When it comes to girls, it's a little different. Can I tell? Should I tell? When should I tell? Should

---

10. An ally is someone who supports and advocates for a community other than their own.

I just not say anything at all because it's not going to work out and she's going to fuck me over? It gets exhausting to think about.

It's been difficult to figure out how to date people, how to approach them, and how to be a single straight dude. In college, it didn't really matter. Most of the people there knew I was trans anyway, and most of the girls didn't really care either way. I don't know if there are fewer options here or I've just gotten pickier as I've gotten older. Part of the problem with passing and being stealth is that lesbian-identified women don't want to talk to me. Even when I do befriend a lesbian, she never thinks of me in that way. The issue with straight girls is that they don't necessarily want to date me either. I look like a guy, I sound like a guy, I am a guy, but then I take off my pants and it's a different situation.

Trying to navigate those frustrations by myself is not an option. I have to be able to vent to my friends or roommates, or call up my trans friends who know what I'm going through. I don't think I could survive up here without a support system.

You Can't Do It Alone

Body image is an important element of how people view themselves. Issues of body dysphoria often lead to poor body image in trans communities, and celebrating a diversity of bodies can help to combat negative body image.

MOSLEY

Being a person of color, I'm shaped a little differently than the white supermodel ideal. Not all clothes are cut for my body. My activism is about being thoughtful, intentional, and comfortable in my body, which is a radical act in and of itself. As trans men and masculine-of-center people, we need this understanding and ownership of our bodies, of what those bodies look like, how we would like to adorn them, and how we feel about our bodies.

We need to focus on empowering people who are all shapes and sizes and who wear all kinds of shit. Giving people different models is so important. That personal sense of ownership of who you are will reflect in your style because you have to be damn courageous to get up every day, to go into the men's section, to buy clothes that aren't necessarily representative of how society tells you that you should dress, to walk down the street, to go to a job interview in that attire, to go to the church in that wear, or go to class. We need to affirm those actions and give everyone the resources to empower themselves to be bold. We need to celebrate, because it takes a lot of courage to be you.

LACY

I think one of the reasons I'm not pressing a hormonal intervention is because I'm so comfortable with my body. I can look at myself naked and not have a problem with it. For me, that confidence really relates to sports. I'm an athlete, so I'm not only in tune with my body [but] also comfortable showering and changing in the locker room.

CAMERON

I spent about twelve years running cross-country and track. Because I started so early, I developed a really positive, athletic self-image. I basically ran year-round, sometimes sixty miles per week. I ran straight through college, which was really hard, because it was a completely female team of athletes. I struggled with fitting in to that group. I eventually became very loud and clownish in that atmosphere, which was fun but was a struggle for me.

I continued to run after college, but eventually I stopped completely because my dysphoria was so high in terms of my chest. Wearing a sports bra isn't exactly identity affirming. When you're running, you're really *inside* your body the entire time. You're really, really connected with yourself, and you can't be anywhere else or you will trip and fall. Yet when you're dysphoric, you're really disconnected from yourself. It's nearly impossible to run when you're dysphoric, so for the past two years I haven't been running at all. Even though I've finally had top surgery, I haven't started running again. I'm nervous about how it will make me feel, because it became tied up with a lot of different feelings toward the end.

DIANE

People are disgusted by the idea of fat people being sexual. A fat friend and I went into an adult store to buy some gag gifts for a bachelorette party. The cashier was friendly, but other people in the store gave us dirty looks. Every eye was following us, wondering what two fat girls could possibly want in a sex store. Surely someone as obese as me can't want to have sex, right?

One of the stereotypes about fat people is that they're asexual. Well, some fat people *are* asexual. To me, "asexual" is a sexuality. I want to have the agency and power of claiming that label. Society lumps fat and disabled people into a category of sexual misfits. They are a group that we consider to be nonsexual, so we label them asexual, which takes away from the individual people within that group who actually do identify as asexual. I am very proud to claim a label as a fat, asexual woman of color, regardless of how uncomfortable that may make others feel.

While a positive body image can lead to increased self-esteem, a negative body image can lead to issues such as disordered eating and depression.

SUPRIYA

Eating disorders are prevalent amongst trans people. Many people need a sense of control over their lives, and as trans folk, they are often given very little. There are a great number of trans men and trans women who come into my clinic who are anorexic or bulimic. Trans men sometimes use extreme weight loss as a way to cease menstruating before they begin hormone replacement, or if hormones don't stop their menstrual cycle.

I moved to Boston to transition. I knew that I wasn't going to have any luck if I stayed in Alabama, and I thought that I'd be able to transition more easily in a big place. I started going to a therapist to begin the transitioning process, and she noticed my low weight. She started asking me questions about how much I ate, how much I weighed, and how often I exercised. She said we could continue to meet and work toward my transition, but she wanted to put me on a diet as well.

I didn't realize how many body issues I had until I realized how reluctant I was to start my diet. I had just needed something in my life that I could control, and since I wasn't in charge of how long it would take to transition I clung to my obsession with counting calories and limiting how much I ate. When I saw my therapist again the next week, I hadn't even bothered to try the diet. She basically told me that she wasn't going to let me transition until I got my eating disorder under control.

That was the slap in the face that I needed to get serious about my anorexia. I wanted to transition so badly, and I was willing to do anything to be able to get on T. I started going to an eating disorder support group every week. Everybody there is coming to the table in a state of vulnerability. There is a sense of connection in a group like that, because you're all fighting the same inner battle. You share bits of your soul, and you get really close with everyone else there. In that group it didn't matter that I was trans. Everyone was really supportive of me and helped me stick to my diet so that I could transition.

I was finally able to gain weight and to start taking T, and I'm so glad that I met my therapist. I know a lot of people want to transition as quickly as possible, but a less attentive therapist might have let me pass through the system without calling me out on my other issues. She treated me very holistically and put me in touch with some truly wonderful people that I'm still in touch with.

VICKY

I struggle with eating. I've been in and out of treatment for eating disorders, but I'm just not able to maintain a diet. If my curves aren't in the right places, I don't want to have them at all. I am still fighting to get on hormones, so I'm trying to pass as a woman without any help. When I'm thinner, it's easier to do that.

ZACH

I have no problems admitting that I'm a fat guy. I was heavy before I was diagnosed with fibromyalgia, and I'm even heavier now. When you hear "eating disorder" you think anorexia or bulimia, but overeating is a disorder too, and it's something I really struggle with.

The interesting thing about being a fat transgender person is that I've been able to experience differences in how fat men and women are treated. As a fat woman I was constantly being picked on. Girls would say really cruel things to me; men would say derogatory things. You go into a department store as a fat woman, and there is no guarantee that they'll even carry clothing in your size. There are a lot of chains that don't make any plus-sized women's clothes. I can't count the number of times some snotty waitress would bring me a diet soda instead of a regular soda, as if it were her job to stage an intervention for my weight.

I've been on and off hormones, and I pass as a guy about half the time. I can always tell if I'm being read as male, because people will never comment about my weight. If the waitress calls me "sir" I know I won't be given a diet soda. When I go into a men's store, they always carry sizes that fit me. It's bizarre how differently we view obesity on men and women, and it's really strange to be on both sides of that coin in the same week.

I went to a restaurant a few weeks back, and the hostess showed me to my table. When she went to seat me in a booth, I asked if I could get a table instead. Booths are hard for big people to squeeze into. She apologized and cleared a table for me without any judgment, and I knew she was reading me as male. The waiter came, and it was clear he was reading me as female. He made a snorting noise when I asked for extra condiments, and he didn't offer to show me a dessert menu. When I left, he called me "ma'am." I'm not old enough to be called "ma'am," but "miss" is a title we reserve for young, thin women.

When I'm in spaces where I'm being read as male, I'm euphoric. But in the many spaces where I'm read as female and belittled for my size or harassed for my sexuality, I'm frequently depressed. We're living at a time and space in history where human beings really treat each other like crap, and we have to have somewhere where we can feel loved and supported. Even more importantly, we have to learn to love ourselves or this world is going to crush us.

Just as trans folk experience high rates of eating disorders, they also have disproportionate rates of depression. These issues are often interconnected and frequently relate to issues like a lack of societal acceptance or body dysphoria.

LUIS
In the fall of my junior year of college, I started calling myself trans, but I used it in the broadest sense of the word. I went back and forth between identifying as trans and genderqueer. Probably my biggest shifts in how I think about myself have come this year. During spring break, I literally just took those ten days to think about my gender. I realized that I'm a trans man, and I want to start transitioning.

My identity was solidified when I came out to my mother. My family is very ignorant, and on top of things, sometimes hateful. My mom isn't hateful anymore, but she's still very ignorant. When I came out to her, I hadn't started transitioning physically yet. The therapist had already written a letter, so it was good to go, but I figured I'd better tell my mom before things went any further. I wrote her an e-mail, but I couldn't press send. I procrastinated by looking at my phone. When I'm in a really deep fit of depression, I take photographs of myself. It's sort of a way to document my depression. I got to one of the darker pictures and thought, do I want to continue to be like this, or do I want to go through the pain of coming out? This pain is greater, I decided. I don't want to be like this anymore.

Prior to coming out, I was definitely suicidal. We can definitely tell how oppressive our society is when we've gotten to this point where there is an entire subset of people who think that suicide is their only way out, or have suicidal tendencies.

BLAKE

Many years ago I tried to kill myself. I was living with an undiagnosed illness that caused me terrible grief; I had so much guilt from leaving my parents and my tribe to pursue my PhD; and there was something wrong with me that I just couldn't put my finger on. At that time it didn't occur to me that I might be a two-spirit. I know there is a history of gender variation among the Mojave, but it's not something that is often recognized these days. Contemporary Mojave culture often neglects tradition, and I never even heard the word hwame[11] until I was taking a Native American studies course as a master's student. Without any way to express the gnawing desire I had festering inside me, I was intimately depressed.

One night all of my feelings got the better of me, and I walked down to a busy overpass. Someone apparently spotted me and followed me as I was nearing it. I hadn't heard him, so I was startled when he called out to me. He said, "Hey! I know what you're thinking about. I've been there before too. Let me buy you a cup of coffee and let's talk."

I spilled my soul to this guy. He is now one of my best friends, and even after thirty years we still get together on a regular basis. When I finally did figure out that I was going to transition, he was the first person I told. Him talking to me that night didn't solve all

---

11. A person assigned female at birth who adopts a masculine role in Mojave culture.

of my problems. I certainly still needed help, but sometimes all it takes is just one person reaching out, and that can be enough to sustain you.

Like Blake and Owen, Juanita likewise found a sense of community through attending a support group.

JUANITA

I go to an HIV support group. At first I went because I had a lot of questions, and I was really depressed. Now I go because these people are my family. It's important to find other people who really get what you're going through. It doesn't matter how strong you think you are, when you're going through something this big you can't do it alone.

CATHERINE

I've been able to get through all of the tough parts of transitioning because I have an amazing support network. My partner and I are members of a motorcycle community, and that's our family. We support one another, and we use a lot of humor to get through. I have a friend who has just recently started to come to terms with her alcoholism. She's no longer in denial, but she's really been depressed about it. Her trope lately has been, "Oh no, I'm so terrible, I'm an alcoholic, there's something wrong with me, people think I'm crazy."

I shook my head and told her, "Look, honey, alcoholism isn't that crazy; I paid someone to cut my dick off."

I think that put things into perspective for her.

Gallows humor is frequently used by trans folk as a way of coping with the negativity, oppression, and fear that they frequently experience.

KURTIS

As with most issues that are too depressing to think about, we have to find the humor in any given situation and relate over the depressing commonality of our experiences. Gallows humor is how trans people survive.

The thought of aging as a transgender person is really difficult. What happens when you go into a nursing home? Will your body be a surprise for the people who work there? Will they treat you with respect and dignity? Trans people think so much about gendered situations like going to the bathroom, and while the idea of becoming incontinent is unpleasant for anyone, it is even more frightening for trans folk. No one wants to have to have somebody help them change their diaper. Nobody wants to lose the autonomy of being able to go to the bathroom by themselves. However, as we age, it's a reality that many of us will have to face.

One day, three other trans men and I were sitting around my living room talking about issues of trans aging. Even though we're in our twenties, it is something we've already started thinking about, a fear that we already have. We were discussing what would happen if we ended up in a nursing home. We all pass really well as male, so the nurses would undoubtedly be confused if they had to change our geriatric diapers. We came to the conclusion that when we get older, we'll print up T-shirts that say, "I have a surprise for you in my pants" on the front. On the back they'll say, "And I shit myself."

ALEXANDER

My partner and I recently did some traveling, and while we were gone we had a house sitter. We have a large dog and a cat, and we wanted somebody to stay in the house with them. I suspect that our house sitter has probably snooped around a bit, and I don't blame her. It's not something I have a problem with; I assume that everyone has a bit of curiosity about other people's dirty laundry, so to speak. The house sitter didn't know that my husband and I are both trans, though she probably does now. [laughs]

Between finding paperwork that may have an incorrect name on it, or finding a drawer full of dildos, I imagine she may be pretty confused. I think that finding out that the people you house-sit for are trannies is the natural consequence of curiosity. I haven't talked to her since then, so I don't know if she snooped, but if she did, she definitely got more than she bargained for.

CATHERINE

One night I was reading the website of the person who created the transgender symbol. She had information about why she did it, why she chose the color, why the edges were round, and so on. The website said something like, "Some people think that trans people are the bridge between men and women. Other people think we're here to bring peace to the world. And of course, other people think that wheatgrass enemas are a good thing."

I involuntarily spit whatever I had been drinking all over the computer and all over the desk. We can just take ourselves way too seriously.

Whether trans folk seek LGBTQI communities, geek cultures, religion, support groups, or other communities all together, the necessity of finding supportive community is apparent.

MOSLEY

Having a sense of community is vital. When you're queer, the world is actively, actively trying to get you to be anything other than who you are, so we need to provide spaces that get us to feel comfortable in our own skin. Having a sense of self [and] a sense of health and wellness is going to translate into all facets of our lives. If we feel worthy, if we feel empowered, [and] if we love ourselves, that's going to show up in our style, in the workplace, in our relationships, and [in] the way we treat others. It's going to show up in how successful we conceptualize ourselves as being.

What Happens to Those of Us with Multiple Identities?

Intersectionality[1] is the idea that multiple facets of a person's identity simultaneously intersect and that individuals experience oppression based on these intersections. Race, gender, sexuality, ability, and socioeconomic status are a few of many identity attributes that co-exist and interact with one another as various elements of a complete whole and are inextricable from one another. For example, Supriya stated, "I am always simultaneously a woman, and a woman of color, and a trans woman."

Within LGBTQI communities, intersectionality can be a site of unity or a source of contention. LGBTQI individuals exist within every race, ethnicity, and religion; they come from all socioeconomic backgrounds and have varying (dis)abilities. Commonality is often overlooked, and there are major fractionalizations based around identity politics, respectability politics, and community goals.

Many individuals who transition experience a noticeable difference in the ways in which they are treated by others, based on their genders. Trans men often experience many aspects of male privilege after transition, while trans women frequently encounter sexism or misogyny. Genderqueer and other nonbinary individuals range in experiences depending on how their gender is perceived by others.

---

1. An idea originally theorized by Kimberlé Crenshaw and used frequently in gender and race studies discourse.

HILLARY

I transitioned in college, and my experiences in the classroom are definitely different than they were before. Prior to transition, my chemistry lab partners for assignments were usually men. After, other men didn't want to work with me. If I did have a male lab partner, he would always talk really condescendingly to me.

In one instance I was working with a real prick of a guy. He had made a mistake in one of his formulas, so I pointed it out to him. He assured me that his formula was correct because he had used "man math" that I "couldn't know anything about."

I shrugged and let him continue with his incorrect formula. It wasn't long before our test tubes were bubbling over with noxious chemicals. I raised an eyebrow and asked if he still thought his formula was correct. He called me a bitch and said I should have been more assertive if I knew his formula was wrong. As a woman in the sciences, situations like this have become all too commonplace.

ERIK

Any woman on a college campus is aware of the high threat of sexual assault. When I was a freshman, I was told where all of the blue-light phones were located. Like the other young women, I could probably still name the locations of all of them. I was taught to walk with my keys between my fingers after dark, and I took multiple women's defense classes during my freshman and sophomore years. I transitioned physically at the beginning of my junior year. By mid-November I was being read consistently as male.

I will never forget the first time I walked home alone after dark after transitioning. As a habit, I had my keys between my fisted fingers as I got off the bus and started the half-mile trek back to my apartment. I passed a group of guys walking the other direction, and they all gave me the unspoken "bro" head nod. In their own silent guy language they were saying, "'Sup, dude?"

I realized that I could put my keys away. No one was going to drag me off into the woods and rape me. Yes, men can be sexually assaulted, but the likelihood of a man being randomly targeted by a stranger is incredibly low. I felt so incredibly liberated in realizing that I could walk wherever I wanted, wearing whatever I pleased, and I didn't have to think about where the nearest blue-light phone was.

My euphoria at this newfound male privilege only lasted a few blocks. As I strolled up the street, I saw a young woman walking down the sidewalk in the opposite direction. As we neared one another, she crossed the street and continued on her way. My emotions did a one-eighty as I realized that she was afraid of me. Me: a trans man who had survived sexual assault, who had participated in Take Back the Night, and organized the campus Week without Violence. I was now viewed as a potential rapist and as a threat to women's safety. It was the first of many times that a woman would cross the street so as to not be forced to walk by me at night, and each time it happens my heart breaks a little more.

Gender privilege and oppression do not occur in a vacuum. Gender is just one of many elements of a person's being, and it intersects with additional aspects of identity such as race and ethnicity.

RAFAEL

There are microaggressions that most of us experience in our daily lives. People make all of these subtle racist, sexist, or classist comments that aren't meant to be offensive but still have the same impact as if they were said with malice. Someone will say something incredibly ignorant and hurtful, but if you call them out, they'll hide behind the excuse that they didn't intend for the comment to be offensive.

I had to reschedule my top surgery. A lot of people will fly to some large city to see a surgeon, meet with them the day before, have surgery, and then stick around until they are healed enough to fly home. This was the case for me. I had my appointment scheduled, but at my presurgery appointment I realized I was going to have to cancel. The surgeon had me take off my shirt so that he could draw the surgical lines on my chest. He became ridiculously flustered because the lines from his dark purple marker weren't visible on my skin. He called a nurse in to ask if they had a marker for black people.

It was really awkward so I tried to fill the embarrassed silent void with questions. I asked him about the possibility of scarring, and he told me, "Yeah, I don't know how your scarring will look. I've never worked on a black person before."

I decided that it would be better for everyone involved if I found a surgeon who had "worked on black people." Top surgeons always have long wait lists, so I was really disappointed that I had to delay my surgery by several months, but I'm so glad I did. My results were great, and I didn't pay thousands of dollars to a surgeon who didn't even have a marker that could draw on my skin.

SUPRIYA

Race and gender are always intersectional issues. I am always simultaneously a woman, and a woman of color, and a trans woman. I moved to the United States from India fifteen years ago to become a doctor, and I am currently in the very, very slow process of obtaining citizenship. My race and my nationality play a major role in how other people perceive and treat me, just as my gender does.

When I first moved to the U.S. as a man, I was treated with a certain amount of respect: when I took my car to the mechanic, he explained the issues to me in detail; I was very rarely interrupted when I was speaking; [and] if I made a mistake, no one blamed it on my gender.

I hadn't yet started my transition when September 11 happened. I saw a marked increase in the hostility I faced. Even though India is a part of Asia, I was viewed as Middle Eastern in the U.S. People were suddenly suspicious of me: I was a dangerous man with dangerous intentions. Since 9/11 I have been pulled over more often, had my bags searched at the airport more often, and been verbally harassed while walking down the street. Between 9/11 and when I transitioned the next year, I was called a terrorist more times than I can count.

Interestingly, once I started being read as a woman, the terrorism comments stopped. Middle Eastern and Asian women are not terrorists; we are objects. Since I transitioned I am no longer accused of being a Jihadist or refused service at restaurants. However, I am catcalled on the street at least once each week; I am constantly interrupted when I speak; my mistakes are always blamed on being an "incompetent woman"; and mechanics won't give me the time of day. Sexism is a daily part of my life now, and it is always colored with racism.

ALEXANDER

I cannot tell you the number of times men made horribly inappropriate comments to me as a woman. There is absolutely no doubt that Western men fetishize Asian women, and I was subjected to their lewd comments constantly. I learned to stay away from frat parties because some asshole would always ask me if my vagina was just as "slanty" as my eyes, or something just as racist and vulgar.

The stereotypes for Asian men are different. Now that I've transitioned I'm not sexualized like I was before, but I certainly still hear a lot of racist comments. Now the "jokes" always focus on cooking cats or driving a taxi. A few weeks ago someone said I shouldn't be allowed to have a cat because I would chop it up and sell it at my Chinese restaurant. First of all, that's an incredibly offensive thing to say, and second, I'm Vietnamese!

RAFAEL

I mostly identify as masculine of center or stud. These terms incorporate not only gender identity and expression but also race, which is really important to me. As an interracial individual, I try to stay away from terms like "transexual" and other identity labels that have been traditionally used in white communities. I see myself as an amalgamation within the matrices of identity: I am masculine of center, and also a person of color, and also queer. I need terminology that addresses all of these aspects because all of those things come together to shape my experience.

I find very often that I end up being the spokesperson for entire communities by virtue of being the only person in those communities. I'm Latino, I'm black, I'm MOC,[2] and I'm often asked to speak for each of these communities in turn. That's not how it works. I'm not here to educate you, nor should anyone be forced to play the spokesperson for an entire group of people. We need more coalitions, more diversity, and more allies to bear some of the burdens of educating others.

GREG

My college has centers for different groups of students. We have a Chicano/Latino center, a black student center, an LGBT center, a disability center, a Native student center, a Middle Eastern student center, and a center for Asian American and Pacific Islander [AAPI] students. All of the centers are in the basement of the student union building. It's great because all of the centers leave their doors open, and one of the centers almost always has food, so students wander among the centers and get free food and make friends with people from different centers.

The problem is that these centers are physically separated. What happens to those of us with multiple identities? Each day I always have to make a decision about where I want to spend my time. Am I more Pacific Islander today or more queer? In the AAPI student center I run the risk that other students won't accept my queer identity. In the LGBT center I constantly encounter racism. I float back and forth between the centers, but it drives me crazy that in this day and age the idea that someone might be interracial and queer, or queer and disabled, or nonwhite and disabled is not something that people can get through their skulls.

---

2. Masculine of center. See glossary.

MOSLEY

As an assistant dean and advisor to black students at Dartmouth College, my position falls under the Office for Pluralism and Leadership. We have offices for black, Latino, pan-Asian, and Native students as well as for LGBT, international, and first-generation students. Having these offices separated can be problematic because it is counter to how I believe identity development works: development is not siloed, and it does happen across identity. The academy is starting to recognize that identity is more nuanced, and the idea of intersectionality is starting to show up in more places, but we have a long way to go for the ivory tower to catch up.

As an institution, we have to meet the needs of the student population of the community, and we're currently in a time and space where we need those separate offices. It would be nice if there were centers, or one area where students could have their needs met across intersectional identities. The current structure doesn't lend itself easily to students who have multiple identities because we have one student who could literally be in every single one of these offices. We're not there yet. I have colleagues who are on the same page as me, so we attempt to do a lot of cross-advising, and a lot of supportive mentoring across those needs for students. For now, there is absolutely a value in having separation there, even if it can be problematic.

KURTIS

As a white trans man, I have a ridiculous amount of unearned privilege. I have privileges based on my race, my socioeconomic status, my gender, and the fact that I'm able-bodied—just to name a few. As soon as people started viewing me as a man, I stopped being sexually harassed. No one has catcalled at me on the street; no one has dismissed my opinion based on my gender. I work in a traditionally masculine occupation, and I'm able to earn raises and promotions because everyone assumes that I'm male. Women in my occupation earn less money for the same work. It's an outrage, and it's the result of living in a patriarchal society.

Race and gender are inextricably connected, which means that I'm not just a man; I'm a white man. As a white guy I don't deal with discrimination, with racial profiling, or with stereotyping. If I'm angry, people don't say, "He's an angry black man"; they say, "Kurtis must be having a bad day." I've never been pulled over or harassed on the street because of my skin tone. I can fill out an application for a house, a car, or a loan, and I won't face rejection or additional screening. This is race privilege, and it permeates every aspect of my life.

As a result of transitioning, I woke up one day as a white man in America. I feel that it's my responsibility to do something with all that privilege, so I decided to work for a racial-justice organization. I do my best to use my powers and privileges to dismantle racism, classism, homophobia, and transphobia. I try to listen to those who are marginalized by racism and help ensure that their voices are heard. I'm not trying to sound chivalrous or gallant. The reality is I have power as a white "dude," and if I'm not actively working toward antiracism, then I'm perpetuating a system of inequality. I can't let that happen.

For trans folk, the ways in which their identities intersect with their socioeconomic statuses often control whether or not they have the resources to physically transition should they decide to do so, or to express their genders in the ways that are most authentic to them.

ZACH

My partner and I are both trans, and we both want to be on hormones and have surgeries, but it's not something we can afford. I came out about five years ago, and I don't even have a letter from a therapist yet. I don't have insurance, and I sure as hell don't have the money for a therapist. I think my partner would be so much happier if he were on testosterone and if he could get top surgery, but unless we win the lotto, that is definitely not going to happen.

For a while, I had insurance through my job. It wouldn't cover any transitional care, but I had an appointment scheduled with a therapist. I was so excited to be making progress toward transitioning. A week before my appointment I got laid off, so I never went in. Now I have insurance again thanks to the Affordable Care Act, but unfortunately my policy still doesn't cover hormones or surgery. My partner and I will both be able to start therapy now, which is a step in the right direction.

We have a jar that we put all of our spare change in. We really want to save up so that we can afford hormones when the time comes. I'm not sure it's going to happen for us though, 'cause the car just broke down again. We don't have a working phone, either, so it's hard to know what to prioritize. Do we save up for testosterone, which we need to be happy, or do we save up for propane so we don't freeze to death this winter?

We're both in jobs that barely allow us to scrape by, and there isn't a lot of room for promotion. We'd like to go back to school, but we can't enroll if we're delinquent on our student loans. We're way behind on our payments. We don't have a phone anymore, so at least the collectors have stopped calling! [laughs] The only way we're ever going to get ahead in life is by winning the lottery. I buy a ticket every week. Some say it's a waste of money, but if you never play you can't win. The thought of winning is what gets me through, even if it is a long shot.

JUANITA

My transition doesn't fit in to some neat idea of how people are supposed to get on hormones. I started out with stolen estrogen and went from there. The only reason I'm able to stay on hormones is because I'm in San Fran and the clinics here really get it. They'll treat any old freak. All of the trans women and the street kids and ladies turning tricks are taken care of. If I were anywhere else I know I'd be screwed, so I'm really glad I live where I do.

KURTIS

Even though I came out when I was only fifteen, I wasn't put on hormone blockers. The technology certainly existed, but puberty-suppressing hormones are very expensive. Our family existed well below the poverty line; there was no way we could afford expensive medications, even though it would have been the best option for me.

MOSLEY

Class is often the most invisible facet of identity. I have a mixed background in terms of socioeconomic status. When I was growing up, my father worked in a factory and my mom went to school. We started with a lower socioeconomic status, had a really working-class experience, and lived in a working-class community. Once my mother was able to attain education and ultimately get her PhD, we were able to change our financial status. We literally had the "moving on up" situation.

Being at an Ivy League institution is privilege personified. We have students who are really intimidated by that but go to great lengths to pass in terms of socioeconomic class.

HILLARY

The LGBT students at my college were divided into cliques. It didn't matter which clique you were a part of; you had to have money. It's amazing to me that queer is this identity that has been so highly commoditized. You must adorn yourself with rainbows, and you must only eat at queer-owned, sustainable, organic cafés, and you must wear Andrew Christian brand underwear if you want to be a part of the group. Do you know how much Andrew Christian costs? It's *underwear* for crying out loud!

A lot of times when you're trans, you're working so hard to figure out all of these new gender cues and roles that you didn't internalize as a child. Oftentimes, trans folk are terrible at communicating early in transition, because we grew up communicating in very gendered ways. Women are expected to be passive, and men are expected to be blunt. I'm not allowed to be blunt anymore; if I have input, I have to carefully veil it in pleasantries rather than just coming out and saying it. I'm not particularly skilled at this, because it's not something I learned as a child. I was too busy learning to be direct and blunt.

Having to relearn how to communicate led to many situations where I felt very awkward and out of place. I wanted to fit in with my peers, and since my social skills were lacking, I tried to assimilate to them as much as possible. This meant I went to great lengths to ensure that I followed all of their unspoken guidelines for being trendy and chic. I had to pick up extra hours at work each week to be able to afford to functionally remain a part of the clique.

ERIK

I grew up with six people living in a three-bedroom trailer. It was crowded, and we went without a lot, but we were never wanting for love. My family has gone through hard times, but we're incredibly close. As a kid, all of my friends were in similar living situations. We lived in a rural, migrant community where poverty was the norm. In my graduating high school class, there were only four of us who went to college and only two of us who finished our bachelor's degrees.

Even though all of my experiences have been working class, I am effectively middle class by virtue of pursuing advanced degrees. I've lost most of my high school friends, because we have very little in common at this point. We no longer feel that we can relate to one another. People don't think of socioeconomic status as culture, but it is. I feel at odds in fancy situations because I don't know how to behave. Simultaneously, my blue-collar friends view me as an outsider. Many of them are also extremely ignorant on LGBT issues. My friends who have traveled or moved to bigger cities tend to be more accepting than my friends who never left our hometown.

Much like socioeconomic status, religion can play a major role in how trans identities are viewed, both by individuals and by communities.

OLIVIA

I'm a Christian. I haven't missed a week of church since I was six.
I went to Sunday school every week as a child, I was a part of the con-
gregational choir in high school, and I went to Appalachian Bible
College before I became a pastor. God is the most important entity
in my life, along with my family. There are a fair number of people
who think that being a Christian and a trans woman are contradict-
ing identities. I think they just haven't spent enough time talking
to God.

I was originally a pastor at a Baptist church. There were a lot of
great people in my congregation, but I find that Baptists tend to act
less out of the love of God and more out of the fear of hell. I left the
Baptist church after a few years because I didn't agree with the focus
on damnation, and I took a position at the United Church of Christ
[UCC].

In my second year at UCC, the congregation took a vote on
whether or not it would take an open and affirming stance. That is,
they decided whether or not the church would preach acceptance
of homosexuality. At the time, I was still uncertain about my feelings on the issue, and I am ashamed to say that I voted against acceptance. This was a very divisive topic, and when the vote was cast
and the announcement was made that we would become an LGBT-
welcoming congregation, many of our members quit the church. I
realized that if I was going to keep my post I was going to have to
reexamine my thinking.

There are so very many lesbian, gay, and transgender people who
have been beaten with the Bible who come to shun God's love. If I
could preach acceptance and compassion, then maybe I could help
more LGBT people see the light of God. I grappled with the Bible,
and I pored over the meanings of the verses that are commonly
thought to give guidance on homosexuality. The number of times
I reread Leviticus!

Every third Sunday our church played host to an LGBT potluck. I
began going to the potlucks and asking members for their interpre-

tations of Genesis 19 and Leviticus 18:22. A lovely woman named Peggy told me that she had always understood the sin of Sodom to be inhospitality, rather than homosexuality. She has since served as an incredible guide for me on my journey to understand the Good Word.

It is such a blessing that I came to this amazing congregation. My views had been so transformed that by the time my kids came out as gay, I was ready to accept them. If I had any lingering doubts about the morality of homosexuality, they were erased when my children came out. God doesn't make mistakes, right? I started thinking, if God doesn't make mistakes, then my cross-gender feelings couldn't be a mistake either. I think I was supposed to be born a man and learn acceptance and love through the journey of becoming a woman. I surmise that God didn't make a mistake with me; he was just teaching me a lesson. I am a trans woman, and I am a Christian, and that is *not* a contradiction.

FELIPE

My *abuelita*, my grandmother, is Costa Rican and Catholic. Of everyone in our family, her acceptance is what surprised me the most. When I was just a lesbian, she told me I was a sinner. Because I am now a *man* [who] dates women, she can view me as heterosexual. Her view now is that I am no longer sinning; I was just born with a challenge that I needed to overcome.

MIRIAM

I suppose if I had been Catholic I would have confessed wanting to be a girl regularly. As a Jew, Yom Kippur was when I atoned for the sin of coveting all things feminine. I would ask forgiveness for my secret feelings, but since I had no intention of reforming my thoughts or actions, it felt like my atonement was a lie. I was needlessly worried about this as a child, as when I finally did tell my rabbi that I wanted to be a girl, he smiled and recited a blessing I had never heard before. It basically translated as, "Blessed are You, Eternal One, to those who make transformations."

He then told me that there are many blessings and rituals that LGBT Jews have created to mark important moments. When I researched further, I found that there are a group of rabbis who are working on creating and compiling a slew of resources and rituals related to trans lives and transitioning. They call the project Trans-Torah.[3] My local synagogue has been nothing but accepting of my transition, and before my surgery we held a presurgery mikveh, a ritual bath.

Intersectional identities can be difficult to describe. Language can be a limiting factor in expressing trans identities, as well as intersectional identities. At other times, adapting language can be a powerful method for conveying identity.

MOSLEY

I use the terms "boi" and "stud" interchangeably as opposed to "butch." Many times when you talk about the butch/femme dichotomy you mostly see two white women. "Butch" isn't really inclusive of communities that I identify in. Embracing the term "stud" is about embracing my masculinity but also my blackness and aspects of black culture that inform who I am. To me, as my race and gender and sexuality come together, it's not a juxtaposition; it's an integration of who I am.

ERIK

There aren't enough concise words to describe these sorts of sexualities. My partner and I are both attracted to female masculinity, whether that's on butch women or trans men. Transensual is a term

---

3. More information about the TransTorah project can be found at http://www.transtorah.org.

used to describe people who are attracted to non-cis bodies, and I feel like it's a label that works really well for me.

RUSS

I use the gender-neutral pronouns "ze" and "hir." When you hear these pronouns in speech, they sound awkward. When you see them written, they look awkward. To me, that's a political statement. You notice these pronouns, and it leads to questions, which lead to dialogues.

LUIS

My partner and I are both Latino, and we speak a lot of Spanish when we're around each other. You would think that Spanish would be really limiting, because there's no real way to be gender neutral: most words end in a masculine *o* or a feminine *a*. But in fact you can express a lot, and you can be really playful. You can combine words like *hermoso* and *linda*. In writing you can use the "at" symbol to show neutrality at the end of a word. When my partner and I write to one another we always write *novi@*, and when we talk we'll combine adjectives and nouns to create playful phrases: *bonita novio, o guapo novia*.[4]

Sexuality Is So Confusing When It Comes to Trans Identities

When a person transitions, identities around sexuality become extremely unclear. Transitioning might or might not cause a shift in the terminology used to identify a person's sexuality. For example, Felipe identified as a lesbian prior to transitioning and now identifies as a straight man. On the other hand, Rafael identified as stud prior to transitioning, and this identity has not changed for yo. However, the ways in which couples or polys are viewed by others can shift as one person transitions.

---

4. Roughly translated, "beautiful boyfriend or handsome girlfriend."

JAIME

I have a cisgender partner, and we've been together for four years. When we started dating, I was a straight-identified woman. He is a straight-identified man, so my transition has been really complicated in terms of our sexualities. I use male pronouns for my partner, so other people assume I'm a straight woman, and they will ignore a host of gender wrongs to the exclusion of all else. There is an assumption of heteronormativity.[5]

When people perceive me as male, my partner and I get identified as a gay couple. My partner has adjusted to it. He's a geek, and he was physically beat a lot in high school. He was called a fag and a pussy, and the school allowed the harassment to continue. He didn't want to fulfill those names, so he was somewhat uncomfortable with my transition at first. On the other hand he's going to be subjected to a certain amount of that if he wants to be with me.

LACY

I started wanting to have surgery while I was dating a bottom.[6] I've always been a twink,[7] but he was really into thinking of me as the masculine one. I didn't mind topping him, but I always feared that I wouldn't be masculine enough for him. There are problems you can solve in a relationship, and then there are game changers. My femininity was an ongoing issue. His identity was built around his fag status. If I came out as a woman, or an ultra-fae guy even, he felt that it would undermine his fagginess. It was a struggle for him.

I kept stepping back from the gender feelings I had in order to appease him. I stayed on "maybe" for a long time, because the relationship was so important to me. It was a very one-sided compromise, which bred resentment, and I wasn't always the best person I could be in the relationship. I was so committed to that relationship

---

5. The idea that heterosexuality is the norm. See glossary.
6. Identity label that indicates preference for a particular sexual role. "Top" is the opposite identity and role. See glossary.
7. Usually a young gay man with very little body hair and a slender frame.

that I wasn't taking care of myself. You have to take care of yourself first, even if it makes other people uncomfortable. Even though we struggled a lot, at least he was honest. He acknowledged that he didn't know if he could be the right person for me, so we ended it.

My current relationship is wonderful. We got together right after I got my implants. He's been very good about engaging in discussions about what has changed in the ways other people perceive me because I'm very excited and want to talk about it. I have to pinch myself sometimes because he sees me so much for who I am. It's a compulsion to ask him, "Are you sure, are you sure?"

Sometimes I feel like it's unreal. He identifies as queer, and he's dated all across the sexuality spectrum. My identity affected my previous partner so much. My new partner isn't deeply affected, because he is so comfortable in his own sexuality and identity, and he seems to have a much better understanding of differentiation. That is, he realizes that no matter how my self-identity may change, it does not affect the way he identifies. I'm my own person, and he is his own.

QUINN

I started dating this woman, Holly, last October. We graduated together from Wesleyan this spring. The first time that we hooked up we were making out, and she stopped me all of a sudden and said, "I'm not really sure how I identify sexually. I hope that's okay with you."

I told her that as long as she was attracted to me, I didn't really care how she identified. I still don't even know how I identify. Prior to dating me, Holly had only had relationships with cismen, so it was pretty validating to have her want to sleep with me. It means that she sees me as a man, rather than as a hairy lesbian. [laughs]

HUGO

Sexuality is so confusing when it comes to trans identities. I currently work two jobs, and my sexuality has come up at both of them in various ways. One of the jobs I started before I began my transition, and all of my coworkers still see me as female. They know I have a husband, so they assume I'm a straight woman. At my other job, I made an offhanded comment the first day about my husband. Apparently they were reading me as male, because they all said, "Oh, so you're gay."

My partner passes very well, and everyone always thinks he's a man. I however do not pass as well. For the most part, I look like a chubby Peter Pan. I'm not complaining: Peter Pan is a total twink. People often assume that I'm a little boy. It makes my husband feel very awkward at times. They sort of assume he's a pedophile, since I look and sound significantly younger than him, despite the fact that we're the same age.

My husband is basically a bear.[8] People will see him and assume that he would either be with another bear or a really skinny twink. When they see me they think, "What the hell?"

I may look young, but I'm certainly no twink. It leads to a huge amount of questions that he hates. He just wants people to accept that we're husbands, no further questions. He has somewhat of an aversion to holding my hand in public. He is very aware of how other people view us, whereas I do not. I love him, and I am so excited to be with him that I forget how we look to other people. I'm so comfortable with myself now that I just don't notice it. However, he is always looking out for our safety. When we get strange looks on the street, it's a good reality check. "Oh, right, this is how other people see us."

There is often overlap between sexual-identity communities and trans communities. Within those spaces, however, there are varying levels of acceptance and education around issues of gender identity and expression, and certain sexualities might be less understood or welcome. Asexuality is one identity that many LGBTQI communities

---

8. Often a large, muscular gay man with copious body hair. See glossary.

tend to ignore or marginalize. Even within LGBTQI spaces, asexuality is often extremely misunderstood.

ALEXANDER

Asexuality is defined as the lack of desire, whereas many other queer sexualities are defined by the existence of desire. For a long time I was in denial about being asexual, because I thought I just had a low sex drive. Everyone says when you start testosterone your sex drive increases, so I figured once I started taking T everything would work out.

I got my first prescription, and after a few months there was still no change in my sex drive. I had hoped that the testosterone was going to be a magical solution, and I wouldn't have to come to terms with my asexual identity. I kept waiting, and waiting, and waiting to become as virile as James Bond. That, of course, did not work. After I had been on testosterone for a year, I realized I was still asexual and knew I was going to have to start coming out to myself and others.

While gay and lesbian and even bisexual are concepts that people can usually wrap their heads around, being asexual is still obscure and very rarely talked about. I have a very difficult time explaining my sexual identity, and it's been very frustrating. On the complete opposite side of the sexuality spectrum, people like Michael Hutchence and David Carradine have managed to make "autoerotic asphyxiation"[9] a household term, but somehow, we still can't talk about asexuality.

KELLY

I spend a lot of time at my campus LGBT center. I guess I'm conventionally attractive, and it always comes as a surprise to people when they find out that I'm asexual. There was a girl sitting along

9. Autoerotic asphyxiation refers to the practice of choking oneself in order to heighten sexual arousal while masturbating. Both Michael Hutchence and David Carradine are said to have died of accidental suffocation as a result of this practice.

the table, whispering to her friend about me. I'm not sure how the conversation started, but I heard her friend say, "No, she's asexual."

The first girl replied, "Really? What a waste."

I didn't say anything because I was dumbfounded. First of all, what was the waste? Do they think it's wasteful not to exploit an attractive body? I don't owe you anything, and you are not entitled to my body. Even if I were sexual, who's to say I would go out with you? Secondly, no human being is a waste. We all have intrinsic value. This is the sort of shit that we hear outside of the community; how dare you bring it inside the community?

The queer community bases so many of its activities around sex. When you walk into the resource center and students are talking about which flavor of condom is their favorite, I know I can't participate. It never even occurs to them that their conversation might be making some people uncomfortable. While their identity seems to be based around their sexuality and sex lives, mine is not. This fixation with sex is a constant presence in many queer spaces, so after a while you feel less and less welcome there. I don't necessarily feel like I fit into the queer community, but I definitely can't find anywhere that I fit out in the heterosexual world.

DIANE

My friends know that I have problems with physical touch in general. Explaining this to one of my best friends was really difficult. I don't think much of binaries, and he loves binaries. He's very well meaning, but binaries make sense to him, so he clings to them. When I told him I was asexual he said, "Are you asexual because you don't like to be touched, or do you not like to be touched because you are asexual? Do you think that if you got used to people touching, you wouldn't be asexual anymore?"

I said, "I don't know. Even if those two things are tied, it doesn't mean it's a problem for you to fix. I like who I am, and I'm comfortable in my identity."

For those of us who are both trans and asexual, there's this idea that our dysphoria is driving our asexuality. There's an idea that once we have surgery, our dysphoria will go away, and we will suddenly become sexual beings. Some people don't even want surgery. Suddenly people assume that you can't really be asexual if you haven't had surgery, as if asexuality and transexuality are mutually exclusive categories.

My partner and I are both asexual, and we're both trans. It's a really nice situation because we can have conversations with one another that are difficult for others to grasp. We both have very similar understandings of what we want, who we are, and what we need in a relationship. We're both still exploring our gender identities and sexualities, but we can do that together in a safe space. One of the most important things that we do is touch base with each other frequently. Are these still your pronouns? Is this still your sexuality? Where do you stand on this? It's important to touch base in any relationship, but even more so when you have multiple intersectional identities.

Survivor identities[10] can also intersect powerfully with both sexuality and gender.

HUGO

My survivor identity impacts my sexuality greatly. I can't have a physical relationship with a biological male. I can't watch porn with men. I can't look at a picture of the male body from the waste down; it terrifies me. My partner wants a hysterectomy? That's fine. He wants to get some form of phalloplasty?[11] That is a huge problem. I love him so much that I would like to hope that I'd be able to cope with changes to his body and we could still be intimate. I love him, not pieces of him. And yet, I have this visceral fear that is so ingrained in me from these past experiences of sexual assault.

---

10. These can be identities developed from experiences of domestic violence, sexual assault, intimate partner violence, or other traumas.
11. A surgery wherein a penis is created. See "genital-reassignment surgery" in the glossary.

I'm a survivor of sexual assault, so I am expected to reclaim my sexuality and reclaim my body. I don't want to do that. I was asexual before and that hasn't changed. Unfortunately, a stereotype of asexual people is that something bad has happened to them and they are afraid of sex and afraid of intimacy. Being a survivor interacts with all of my identities, each in a different way. I don't want to engage in compulsory heterosexuality at all.

It Often Falls on Us to Educate Them About Our Conditions

Having an intersectional identity is very complex. Often our identities are so intertwined it is impossible to separate different parts of the whole. Likewise, the struggles that face both transgender communities and disability communities are often intersectional and inextricable. Disabled and differently abled transgender individuals embody this intricate intersectionality and show just how connected disability and trans identities are.

HILLARY

Although I am deaf,[12] I pass as hearing very easily because I lip read and I don't speak with very much of a Deaf accent unless I'm tired. My parents are not deaf, but there are other deaf people in my family, so I grew up learning to function in both hearing and Deaf spaces. In the Deaf community, we have some bizarre gender policing. Someone will transition and will be harassed for suddenly not signing in a way consistent with their gender. Since I've transitioned, people will say to me, "You're signing in a very masculine way."

I was taught to sign in a certain way. This is my "voice" in the

---

12. The lowercase word "deaf" describes a condition of not hearing, whereas the capitalized word "Deaf" describes a group of deaf people who share common language, culture, social beliefs, and behaviors.

Deaf community. I don't really know how to sign in a more feminine way, and I'm not sure I want to learn. I'm happy with the way I sign, and I shouldn't have to change it because others expect me to sign in the way they think I should.

In the hearing world, I am frequently policed about my voice, which I cannot hear, and I cannot consciously change. I can't. Beside the fact that I don't want to, I don't know what it means to speak higher or lower. For goodness' sake, I can't hear!

BLAKE

I have transverse myelitis,[13] and different days I use different ways of getting around. I was going to try to use crutches today, but I ran into a friend who was having an episode of his disability so I gave one of my crutches away. Today I am in my wheelchair instead. Able-bodied people will come up to me and ask, "What's with the wheelchair?"

"Well, it's what I need. What's with the questions?"

I've noticed that particularly with visible disabilities, your body seems to become public property. People feel absolutely entitled to information about how your body works and what you do with your body. This is very true for trans folk as well. People think they have the right to invade your identity. They ask, "What kind of trans are you? Have you had surgery?" With disabilities, it's the same kind of invasiveness; it's the same kind of right that people think they have to ask you questions that they wouldn't ask anybody else.

Last May, I was taking public transit and I got trapped by a woman who asked me questions about my crutches for forty-five minutes. She asked if my legs were broken, and when I told her they weren't she needed to know why I used crutches, how long I'd been using them, how long I would use them in the future, whether or not there is a cure for transverse myelitis, and so on. I didn't want to tell her

---

13. Transverse myelitis is a neurological disorder caused by inflammation of the spinal cord. It can result in varying degrees of paralysis.

off for asking inappropriate questions because I didn't know how long I was going to be stuck sitting next to her.

People don't understand how hurtful their questioning can be, especially if you're in a place where you haven't had an invitation to learn the skills to provide pushback to that, or you're in a position where you can't push back because of the power dynamics involved. We become paralyzed by others treating us like public property and then we're retraumatized. It's really hard to have the intersectionality of many identities, where people think they have this right to inquire about who you are and ask questions that they normally wouldn't ask.

DIANE

One of the things that often strikes me is this sense of being suspect. I think about what it means to be a *body* that's suspect. For me, I experienced it for a long time as a fat person because I was seen as being the absolute opposite of what it means to be healthy and well, as if wellness is a personality trait in and of itself.

After I was diagnosed with multiple sclerosis [MS] I started to experience people projecting their own fears onto me, as if I was a mirror into their future, instead of a human being. I had a neighbor watch me taking a minute and a half to make my way into a car, and I could see her frown, wondering what the hell that was about. I found out in a later conversation that her look, which I had initially interpreted as judgment, was rooted in her own fear. She knew I had MS and had just been diagnosed herself. She was looking at me and thinking, "Is that going to be me one day?" I was her worst nightmare.

That sense of being public property never goes away. People frequently ask me how long I'm going to be "like this." It's new for them when I walk with a cane or use a wheelchair. People think I'm so suspect that I need to be questioned on the spot and interrogated, because that information must be put out for them. The real question they are asking me is, "How long do I have to deal with your difference?"

As a trans woman, this is nothing new to me. Anyone who performs their gender in a way that others disagree with is treated as suspect. As a person of color, I have been treated as suspect my entire life. I'm so used to being questioned about my gender and my race that in many ways, I have been conditioned to automatically answer invasive questions about my disability when questioned.

Beyond questioning someone about their physical or mental condition, there is plenty of scrutiny that happens around disability, often from people who have little to no connection with disability communities.

ZACH

When I went in for my last interview, I went without my cane. I really need a cane to get around, but I don't use it at work because I'm terrified that I'll be harassed. Usually I'm around a counter that I can hold on to and pretend that I'm fine if I do have extreme pain. I know it's harmful to work without the cane. I'm not trying to be macho; I just want to keep my job.

MIRIAM

I have extreme photosensitivity, which I generally accommodate by wearing sunglasses. Even when I'm inside, if I'm near a window and it's bright out, I have to wear them. People tell me to remove my sunglasses on a daily basis, but if I'm in a sunny room, like in a bank, I cannot take them off and still be able to see. A grocery-store cashier once told me that people are suspicious of where I'm looking. Sorry, I need to see. As long as people aren't being jerks about it, I'll trade out my darker sunglasses for a somewhat lighter pair to try to pass them off as regular glasses, but when I do that I certainly don't see as well.

People make assumptions. For those of us with a visible disability, the presumptions are sometimes louder. I wear my sunglasses during the day because the light is too bright, but I can't see if it's too dark either. One time I was crossing the street. I was out at night with my cane, and someone just came up and grabbed my arm and dragged me across the street. He didn't even say anything. I had to fight the urge to yell because I didn't know what he was doing or when he was going to let go. When we got to the other side of the street he said "UP!" I assume he was trying to warn me that there was a curb, but I tripped because he was making me walk so fast. Then he got mad at me and said, "I tried to tell you!" and that was it. He was gone, and I was standing on the corner just mystified.

On the other end of the spectrum, when I don't have my cane or my sunglasses and I seem to be passing as able-bodied, I'll say that I need help reading a menu because I don't see very well. The waiter will always look at me and say, "Of course you can!" or "No, you're not blind."

Because I can walk out of my house, hold a job, or go shopping, people assume that I don't actually have the disability that I "claim" to have. I meet the legal definition for being blind, but I have learned to make accommodations for myself. The only thing that I really can't do is drive a car. I don't want to drive a car! [laughs] I know I don't see well enough to be safe on the road.

GREG

As a result of my cerebral palsy, I have some paralysis in my legs. I use different modes of aide. I'm in a wheelchair about 90 percent of the time, but from time to time I use a walker. I can't use a walker for very long, and I have to rest frequently. I can stand for about one minute, and I can take about twenty steps and then I must rest for about fifteen minutes. There are some places that I have to go that require me going over curbs, so I can't use a wheelchair. This leads to people seeing me one day in a walker and one day in a wheelchair, and they assume I'm faking my disability.

It seems more often than not that when I go to the supermarket I'm invisible. People walk right in front of me. They don't seem to realize that once I get going in this chair, I can break your ankles really quick. I wear leather gloves as a stopping gauge, and I can't tell you how many pairs of gloves I've gone through from having to stop immediately in order to not run into someone. Have you ever used your hands as breaks? I'm considering putting an old-fashioned bicycle horn on my chair. It seems like it might be effective.

There are many types of disabilities, but most are frequently classified into the broad categories of invisible or visible. Visible disabilities might be indicated by the use of a wheelchair or a cane. Invisible disabilities might be those pertaining to mental-health or physical-health issues that are concealable. Those with visible and invisible disabilities each face a different set of struggles. Sometimes those struggles overlap; at other times there is little commonality.

HILLARY

A mental disability, while not visible, is something that can be just as debilitating as a disability that is seen. Because autism is invisible, I often can't get accommodations at work.

BLAKE

There are different issues with visible and invisible disabilities. When I just had invisible disabilities, I definitely had the privilege of not being harassed or discriminated against in the overt ways that I am now when I'm primarily in a wheelchair. Before, I thought of myself as an ally to the disability community, and thought I understood, but nope! I had no idea whatsoever. I find now that I get a lot more acknowledgment from the general populace. They see my wheelchair and say, "Oh, of course you're not working right now," which is a double-edged sword: I'm actually working more now.

RUSS

Most of the time, I function fairly well in hearing spaces, but I had a situation at work where I decided to use an interpreter. I work for an LGBTQ advocacy firm, and we were mingling at a social event where we were supposed to ask people for donations. I figured if I had to ask people for money, I needed to hear what they were saying. A board member, who had been previously very friendly to me, came up to me to start talking, saw the interpreter, and turned around and went the other way with a disgusted look on his face.

I feel so much guilt and shame when I ask for interpreters because I feel like my deafness is not as deaf as the other person's deafness. Just like not trans enough, we have not deaf enough in the Deaf community. I feel like because I hear some, it's not 100 percent necessary to have an interpreter, because I would get about 50 percent of what you're saying. I feel bad that I'm asking for this help to get from 50 to 100, and people often reinforce my feelings of guilt by acting like it is a huge burden to get me an interpreter. I rarely use interpreters because they are seen so much as a barrier. People see the interpreter and no longer see me; my disability goes from being invisible to visible.

I'm often in kinky play spaces,[14] and one time I happened to have an interpreter with me. Someone came up to the interpreter and asked him whether or not I would like to play.

The interpreter was horrified. He turned to me and signed, "I'm not negotiating your scene for you! What the hell?" [laughs]

Disabilities intersect with trans identities in both overt and subtle ways. Understanding these intersections is an important part of creating community-wide dialogues and generating greater harmony.

VICKY

When I tell other people in the trans community who know that I have schizoaffective disorder that I want to transition, they don't take me seriously. We have this overt policing in our own house, in our own communities, [and] in our own subcultures. Before we can have a good conversation about intersectionality, we have to recognize the idea that people can have more than one disability.

---

14. A space where people meet to negotiate and engage in sexual activities.

ZACH

Even though fibromyalgia affects men, 75 percent of the people it affects are female. It's one of those things where I'd rather not have it be known that I have fibromyalgia, not because it's a disability but because it might tip people off that I'm trans.

DIANE

I find that disabilities compound along axes of dis-privilege. One of my friends is a ciswoman who is pregnant, which is a temporary disability, whether or not we think of it in those terms. She gets asked a lot of really invasive questions about her pregnancy. Complete strangers will come up to her and touch her stomach, and that baffles me. Men do not touch each other. As a trans woman, I get a lot of unwanted touching, which is something that I hate. Men in many cultures don't touch each other much, but as a woman now I'm touched all the time by both women and men, and it drives me crazy.

GREG

It troubles me that we can't make a universal bid at accessibility. There are so many levels of disability, and we battle within the disability community about invisible versus visible disabilities. We need to be working with one another instead of fighting for the title of more-disabled-than-thou.

The last conference I was at had only a five-minute break between sessions, and the bathroom was on the other side of the convention center. I tried to point out this dilemma to one of the conference managers, and he retorted that the conference was completely ADA compliant.[15] I told him that it may very well meet the legal definition of compliance, but true accessibility goes beyond just the obvious issues like holding a conference in a location without stairs; [in addition, it involves] giving attendees enough time to eat, hav-

---

15. Americans with Disabilities Act.

ing tables that are short enough that people in wheelchairs can set their food, ensuring that the food isn't full of allergens, and making sure the bathrooms are accessible. He told me that if I needed to, I could use the special staff-only bathroom. It was a one-person solution, but it wasn't as if I was the only disabled person. Yet, when a disabled person brings up these issues, people will act so defensive. When a trans person brings up the issue of a gender-neutral bathroom, people go completely ballistic.

This is not just an issue for people with disabilities, and it's not just an issue for trans folk. We all need to pee. That's the takeaway here. [laughs]

Beyond the similarity of needing accessible restrooms, and the social stigma of being treated as public property, trans folk and people with disabilities share similarly complicated barriers when attempting to access health care. Disabled trans folk often face difficulty in finding providers who are knowledgeable about their disability and their gender identity.

BLAKE

My disability went undiagnosed for many, many years. What people know about this illness is really squat. When I was first diagnosed, I knew more than my PCP [primary care physician], so I told him, "I need you to get educated and I need you to make that commitment to stay up to date on the research about my disability and about my disease or we are not going to work together. I will go find somebody else, if I need to."

He's been great, though. As luck would have it there is a specialist in transverse myelitis at the university near me, and he's wonderful with my disability but horrible about trans stuff, so I'm really working with him on it. It's a trade-off. Do I need competent health care, or do I want to be treated with respect? There seems to be a weird paradox between knowledge and respect, and it seems like the specialists I've seen are incapable of having both.

ZACH

It took forever to get my fibromyalgia diagnosed. It was very sporadic where my pain showed up: sometimes it was in my back, sometimes it was in my feet, [and] sometimes it was in my knee. My primary care doctor suggested that my pain stemmed from my family history of diabetes, or because I was fat. I understand that I'm overweight, but that's a thing I've been dealing with forever. The pain is new.

There was always a constant pain, but I'd get specific pains three or four times per day, and they were bad enough to drop me. There were a lot of things that I thought were normal that weren't. It impacted every aspect of my life, and until I was diagnosed I wasn't able to get any sort of accommodations. Now that my pain is being managed, I can hold a job, but it's still a struggle to get going a lot of the time.

One of the things that can trigger fibromyalgia pains is hormonal imbalance. A lot of people who get fibromyalgia are not only female but in their midfifties and going through menopause. It's possible that my experience of being on T on and off might have caused my fibromyalgia pain. Since I was taking T without a prescription, I haven't mentioned this to my doctor. But from the research I've done it seems plausible.

GREG

The medical system seems to assume that those of us with childhood disorders all die off at eighteen. There are cerebral palsy [CP] specialists and orthopedists in pediatrics that understand my disability and my trans identity. I'm twenty-four, and I'm still seeing my pediatric neurologist. I have to still worry about aging out every time I go. There's hardly anyone who specializes in adult CP, and if they do, they don't seem to have a handle on gender identity.

Additionally, I have to travel in order to see my specialist every few months, which is an insurance nightmare because they don't want to cover me out of a certain area. I got lucky in terms of insurance, because my parents are still covering me. My dad's plan has a clause that allows children with disabilities to stay on it longer. I got lucky. If I hadn't, I definitely wouldn't be able to go to those specialists and I'd be screwed six ways to Sunday.

From struggling to find trans-friendly medical specialists to being treated as suspect and feeling isolated from others, disabilities are incredibly intersectional and can affect daily life to a great extent.

RUSS

When you are deaf, your community is very small. If you are hard of hearing, you don't really belong within the Deaf community or the hearing community. When you are LGBT, your community is also very small, and trans folk are the tiniest part of the community. When you combine the people who are transgender and the people who are part of the Deaf community, you find yourself in the center of one of the teeniest Venn diagram sections. The entire community of people who might possibly understand you is a dot. Now add being a person of color or having a mobility issue to that, and your world becomes even smaller. When you find yourself at the intersection of multiple identities, there are few people to whom you can relate.

ZACH

Fibromyalgia goes hand in hand with chronic fatigue. If I exercise one day, which makes my pain better, I will sleep throughout the entire next day due to chronic fatigue. The other day I exercised, and the next day I slept until 6:00 p.m. When I woke up I thought it was really early because it was so dark out, but in fact, it was very late. I asked my partner what time it was, and I honestly didn't believe him when he told me.

GREG

I had an aide helping me throughout my primary education. I tended to make friends with adults a lot faster than kids my own age, because the teachers had to know what I needed first. Kids thought I was weird because of my mobility devices, and they certainly didn't want to talk to me with my aide there. I never had unsupervised interactions with other kids because there was always an adult with me.

It created a gap where I didn't interact with people my own age, and when I did it was very, very negative. Going through school with braces and crutches was awful. I got beaten to a tar on a regular basis. I remember getting called "metal legs" and "Frankenstein" and "retard" all the time. Nearly every day someone would try to trip me so they could laugh as I struggled to get back up. After a few years of that I didn't want to interact with other kids. I was too scared.

Ironically, I feel right at home in the trans community. There are so many of us who didn't learn to socialize "correctly" as children. Trans kids are either too busy trying to figure out their identities or they are learning how to interact based on their biological sex. Then they transition and have to relearn everything, but their brains are no longer prepared to absorb that information the way they did as children. We're an awkward group, but we're united in our awkwardness, which somehow makes it less awkward.

Many of the individuals I spoke with were involved in activism within both trans and disability communities as a way of finding community and advocating for their rights.

HILLARY

There is a major infantilization of disabilities. Something I get a lot in the autistic world is that I keep aging out of things because there are no autistic people above nine years old. [laughs] Did you know this? It's true. There are so few books on adult autism. The last autism books I read basically said, "It's okay because your kid will be ten forever, but you can still love them!"

It's shocking to me how much the conversation needs to be taken away from this medical and academic infantilization and put back into the hands of people with disabilities.

As I developed my own identity of being a disabled person, it made me start thinking about other folks with other disabilities, and working in the mental-health field, I think a lot about mental-health disabilities. I find myself often being an advocate for people with disabilities other than my own, and the fucked-up part is people think I'm strange.

I'll be somewhere and say, "There are stairs here, and this is a problem for people with mobility issues." The response is always, "Well, you don't have to worry about that."

Yes, I do, because other people do. There's a certain lack of responsibility that people seem to have when it concerns people who can't do the same things that they can do.

BLAKE

There is an astonishing lack of awareness and respect for people with disabilities and for trans people, which means it often falls on us to educate them about our conditions or about other people's conditions. Most people don't know what gender fluidity is, so I'll have to explain that. Most people don't know what transverse myelitis is, so I'm always explaining myself and educating other people about really basic and important parts of who I am. Sometimes I'm too tired to explain, and I shouldn't have to. At the same time, there's a need for education, and you almost have to pick your battles regarding when to educate people and when not to. That's a balance that I really struggle to find, but I feel that this is an issue that is really intersectional between being trans and disabled, and it's a huge part of my activism.

We're Connected in More Ways
Than We Want to Admit

Strictly speaking, disorders of sexual development (formerly called intersex conditions) are not considered transgender identities. However, there is a lot of commonality between intersex and trans issues. Estimates of the prevalence of disorders of sexual development and the prevalence of gender dysphoria are remarkably close, and some speculate that there are hidden connections between the two. Regardless of whether or not a connection exists, both are important aspects of human biological diversity.

ASH

Because of my dad's drug charges, my mom was unable to have custody of me as long as he was around. Even though my dad eventually went to prison, it was too traumatic to be in the house so I never went home again. However, whenever I was in town, home from college, my mom and I would get dinner. It was always awkward, but we did it anyway.

One time, we were at Pizza Hut, eating breadsticks and awkwardly forcing conversation. My mom told me the first dirty joke she had ever told me. Then she got really, really embarrassed and ran to the bathroom. She came back fifteen minutes later and tried to change the subject. I think she was really overwhelmed with her own awkwardness, and she blurted out, "Did I ever tell you that when you were born, you were born with an extra body part and it starts with a C?"

Then she got up, paid the bill, and we left. She ignored that she had ever said it. I kept trying to get clarification, but she kept changing the subject.

About a year and a half ago, I went to Arkansas with my mom. We were visiting family, and it was probably the best that we've ever gotten along. I was the only person on the car-rental contract, so I was the only one who could drive. While I had my mom trapped in the car, I brought up the conversation that we had six years ago. Apparently, when I was born the nurse was giving me a bath and said, "Oh, lucky her. She was born with a double clit. Don't tell the doctor."

My mom was really confused and concerned. She asked if it

would cause any problems. The nurse told her that it wouldn't but warned her again not to tell the doctor because he would make a bigger fuss out of it than it was. She said, "As long as you don't tell the doctor, it will work out well for her in the future." [*laughs*]

My mom didn't ask any further questions because she was a first-time mom and she was so glad to have a child after having multiple miscarriages. In the mid-1980s, information on disorders of sexual development wasn't accessible to most people. My mom didn't spend a lot of time with other girl babies, so I guess she just didn't know what things were supposed to look like.

I've always known that something was a bit different. My reproductive system doesn't work the way that everyone tells me it should. I went to a free clinic to ask about it, and they said they could do a physical exam. They wanted to test for genetic markers, which is really expensive, so they couldn't do it because it is considered a specialty procedure. I tried to do some more research, but "double clit" is a terrifying Google search. [*laughs*] Don't try it without the safe-search filter on.

I realize that my physical anomaly is an intersex condition, which probably has nothing to do with my gender identity. However, I cannot help but wonder sometimes if the two are related. We don't know why people are transgender or genderqueer, but we have a decent understanding of why people are intersex. Trans and intersex communities often want nothing to do with one another, but we're connected in more ways than we want to admit.

We Don't Put Ourselves in Vulnerable Situations Willingly

Discrimination and bias are daily occurrences for many transgender individuals. Whether facing institutionalized oppressions or interpersonal violence, the bias that trans folk encounter can be overwhelming and often leads to exceptionally high rates of suicide and depression.

ERIK

Interpersonal violence is part of life when you're trans. If you're lucky, and you pass well enough, you can often avoid the major violence. If you don't pass well, or you're denied hormones for too long, you're going to get the shit beaten out of you. At the bare minimum you're going to be called terrible names or be verbally harassed frequently. At the other end of the spectrum, you'll be physically beat, likely hospitalized, and possibly killed.

When I was an undergrad, I was out and outspoken in the community. A lot of people knew that I was trans even though I passed, and that put me at risk. I was beaten up on campus in a stairwell of the student union building. It was early evening, and as I entered the stairwell, another guy was coming down. He said, "Wait a minute, don't I know you?"

I didn't get a chance to even look at him before he punched me in the face and called me a "fucking tranny." I fell back, and my head hit the concrete wall, and the next thing I remember I was laying on the ground fifteen minutes later. I reported it to the campus police, but they never caught the guy who did it. I was really lucky that the guy didn't go any further than he did.

HILLARY

I've been called every name in the book. When you're a trans woman, people assume that you are a prostitute and a drug addict. It's a stereotype that hurts everyone, including the trans women who are, in fact, sex workers or addicts. There's this idea that all trans women are worthless, and because of it, we're frequently harassed. I've been refused service at restaurants on a number of occasions, and in a number of states it's completely legal to refuse to serve trans folk.

FELIPE

If you go to a bar, and you get wasted, you're going to do something stupid. When you're trans, that something stupid can be so much more dangerous. I'm sure you can think of all the stupid things that can happen. A big problem is, you may not even remember them the next day. Or maybe you remember what you did, but you don't remember who saw. It could spiral very quickly, so I never drink in public.

When I first moved up to Alaska, I had a couple of what I would consider "close calls." Early on, I tried to pick up someone who was apparently not down.[1] Another time I got drunk and needed to use the bathroom, but there weren't any stalls or doors in the men's room. I figured out really quick that I needed to be more aware.

Now that I'm familiar with the area, I feel little bit better about it. I know where I'm going, I know who I will be with, and I know what the bathroom situation will be like. Even if my friends don't know anything about me being trans, they are at least there to have

---

1. "Not down" means not being open to the idea of having sexual relations with a trans person.

my back. If I get too drunk, they'll stick me in a taxi and make me go home.

CATHERINE

An old friend, five years gone, once said she'd never consider any trans person to be out of danger. Every single trans person has at least one trans friend who has been murdered, taken their own life, or died needlessly because they were too afraid to seek medical care. My friend Julie died just last year because she put off going to the doctor. She was afraid of how she'd be treated. We're terrified, so we don't put ourselves in vulnerable situations willingly, and our small medical problems become really big issues really fast.

Bias and discrimination can come from complete strangers or can be found closer to home. As aforementioned, families do not always provide supportive environments.

LUIS

My dad, who is really bourgeois, and I went to a restaurant in the Strip neighborhood. It's a poor area of Pittsburgh, but it has great food. We walked by a homeless person, and it was very clear that she was trans. My dad walked by and said, "Mira eso" (Look at that; that's disgusting). He was so upset about her presence, and he treated her like slime. Looking back, I thought, "Shit, my dad was really transphobic and classist in that situation."

I'm sure as a young kid that really affected me. You learn how to be a human being from the people immediately around you. I learned masculinity from my dad, and that's not good. He's aggressive, misogynistic, and entitled. I think about my masculinity very cautiously, and I try to be aware of myself. Luckily, I was born a woman: if I had been born a man, I think I would've turned out like my dad.

At other times, violence comes from partners. Many of the characteristics of domestic violence manifest differently in LGBTQI relationships. Because there are so few support services for LGBTQI families, domestic violence is often an issue that trans folk feel they have to deal with on their own.

RAFAEL

My mom raised me to date men. She was so concerned that, as her daughter, I would end up in an abusive relationship like she had. No one had taught her to recognize abuse. As a black woman, she was taught that although her relationship may not be perfect, it was important to present herself to the world as though nothing was wrong. If you tell people about your marriage problems, they will think that all black people have marriage problems. What you do as a person of color is amplified and projected onto an entire community, so you must conduct yourself with dignity and respect, and you can't tell anyone about your problems. These are the ideals that she was taught, and she didn't want me to grow up believing the same things.

It's true that people will project your experience as a person of color onto other people, and it's true that people are going to make assumptions based on race. However, my mom taught me that if I was in an abusive relationship, I should get out of it, no matter what anyone in the community thought about it. She and my father divorced shortly after I was born. He beat her frequently, almost to death a few times. She didn't want me to have to go through that, so she left him.

She taught me from day one that if a man hit me, tried to control me, manipulated me, lied to me, or cheated on me, I should dump his ass and move on. She raised me to be a strong woman, and I appreciate that, even though I'm now a man.

It took me a long time to reconcile what she taught me with the ways that it applied to dating women. Before I transitioned, I was a stud. I dated a number of women, and it took me way too long to realize that some of those relationships were abusive. My mother taught me that power and control is a male problem, that men are the abusers. It never occurred to me that two women could have an abusive relationship. I dated a woman who was extremely manipulative. She always had to know who I was with, what I was doing, where I was going. She read my e-mails and checked my phone. She was constantly checking in on me. Had she been a man, I might have realized earlier that this was an unhealthy relationship, but it never occurred to me that if a woman engaged in these controlling and stalking behaviors, it was still abuse.

I was so unaware that my prior relationship was abusive that I ended up in another abusive relationship. I was dating this girl Marcia, who was black and Latina. I loved being with her because she understood my experience so fully. Finding a space to navigate a mixed-race identity is hard. Then add being a lesbian to that. Now add being trans. Spaces to express all of those identities simultaneously just don't exist, so when you find someone who really understands your experience, you cling to them. I was clinging to Marcia.

Things started off great because we had so much in common, but Marcia soon became wary of my friends. First it was just one friend: "Oh, she really bugs me; I wish you wouldn't bring her over all the time."

I stopped seeing that friend, but it didn't solve the problem. "Why are all your friends so annoying? Why do you need to spend time with them anyway? Aren't I enough for you?"

I thought that maybe she was right. Maybe it was time to settle down and start focusing on my relationship. I cut out all of my friends from my life, but that didn't solve our problems either. "Why do we spend so much time with your family? We never spend time with my family. Can't we skip seeing your sister this weekend?"

Her family lives in Puerto Rico; of course we didn't see them often. I saw less and less of my family, but it didn't solve the problem. Next, it was people I worked with. She was so jealous, so controlling. Little by little she was isolating me so that I had to rely on her and her alone. She began asking me about how I spent my money, criticizing anything I bought. She followed me to the mall one day, and when I confronted her, she said she was meeting me there to surprise me. She read my bank statements. She would say things like, "Why can't I have your e-mail password? What are you trying to hide?"

One night we were arguing about something or other, and she hit me. She smacked me across the face, and it still didn't occur to me that maybe there was something wrong with this relationship. As soon as she did it, she was apologetic.

"I'm so sorry, I just got angry, I'd never really hurt you," she said. We made up, and things were a little bit better for a few weeks. Until she hit me again.

The funny thing is, it wasn't her hitting me that made me realize something was wrong: it was what she said after. She told me not to tell anyone because people would think that all black, Latina lesbians were abusive, and she didn't want to hurt the community. That raised a red flag. That was a tactic of manipulation that my mother had taught me to recognize, and it hit me like a tidal wave. I was absolutely flooded with shock that these words were coming from a woman. A woman was abusing me. How stupid was I that it took me so long to notice?

I waited until she went to work the next morning; then I packed up my things and I left.

We Need More Compassionate Doctors

Violence against trans folk can be overt, such as verbal or physical harassment, but violence and bias can also be much more subtle. Many trans folk feel wary and uncomfortable in medical settings, often due to perceived discrimination or the fear of discrimination.

JAIME

I had to fire my therapist because she told me that my preferred pronouns were too difficult to use. She refused to even try. She told me that since my partner was cisgender I needed to get rid of him because he was going to hold me back in my transition. She told me that if I was really serious about transitioning, I should only be using men's bathrooms. I'm not being read as male often enough to want to put myself in such a potentially dangerous space, not to mention the fact that I don't really identify as male.

She was pushing me to transition way faster and way further than I was really willing to go. I told a friend of mine what had happened, and she told me I should stop seeing that particular therapist. I realized, "Oh yeah, I can do that!"

I cancelled my next appointment and sent her a really long e-mail with a few articles about nonbinary identities.

KELLY

I'm a survivor of sexual assault, and I told my therapist that I think I might be asexual. She replied, "Are you sure you're actually asexual? Or do you think it's because of the trauma that you've been through?"

I told her, "Even if it is because of the trauma that I went through, it's still who I am. It's a valid identity."

Medical doctors will also say the same thing to me. They always want to find the underlying cause of my asexuality. They assume that it's something they can fix. Well, even if it is, I don't want them to fix it. It's part of my identity, and I'm very happy being asexual.

KURTIS

I'm a safer-sex educator. I travel around the country and present on LGBT sexual-health topics. At the end of my workshops I always give out safer-sex supplies. The night before one of my presentations, I realized I didn't have any dental dams.[2] I went all over town looking for them. I went to all of the drug stores, to the LGBT resource room, and to the on-campus pharmacy, and I couldn't find anything. I finally went to the hospital pharmacy. This is a major

---

2. A barrier, usually made of latex, that covers the vagina or anus during oral sex.

teaching hospital, at a major college. I asked the pharmacist who was working if they carried dental dams, and she said, "I don't even know what those are."

I couldn't believe it. First of all, they have a legitimate dental use that a pharmacist might want to know about, and second, they are sort of the bread and butter of queer safer sex. It was upsetting that she was so ignorant because she was a pharmacist, and even more upsetting because she was a woman. It's not like dental dams are just used by queers. I really felt bad for her sex life. [laughs] As a medical professional you need to be able to tell your patients how to stay safe when they're having sex, and for a lot of lesbians and trans folk, a condom isn't the way to do that.

LACY

Being nonbinary is scary. Being a person of color and nonbinary is probably even scarier. I've had so many bad times with doctors; I don't remember which was the worst. I was going to catch the subway one day, and I tripped down the stairs. It's not easy to run in these heels I wear. I fell right at the bottom of those stairs and I felt my leg crack. I knew it was broken the minute I tried to stand on it.

I went into the emergency room, and they didn't make a hurry about seeing me; broken bones don't rank very high next to heart attacks. They finally got me into a room, and this really pale nurse came in and looked at my ankle while she filled out charts and asked me questions. When the doctor came in, he told me he wanted to take an X-ray of my leg. When he left, the nurse asked me when my last period was. I asked her why she wanted to know that, and she said that they don't like to do X-rays if there's any chance I might be pregnant. I told her I don't have periods. She was really confused, so I told her why I don't get periods and her white face got even whiter.

She left the room, and I could hear her in the hallway talking to the other nurses. They were all hushed so I couldn't hear what they were saying, but I knew it was about me.

I sat there and waited. And I waited, and I waited, and I waited.

I didn't have a watch, and there wasn't a clock in that room, so I limped out to the hallway to ask what time it was. Four o'clock. I'd been there since eleven. I wasn't sure what to do, so I went over to the nurse's station and told one of the nurses that no one had talked to me for five hours. That nurse looked at me and said all smarmy, "We've been real busy; we'll get to you soon."

I started walking my gimpy self back to the room, and as I'm leaving I hear another nurse say, "Don't worry, we don't have to treat it."

It! It is what you call a dog. It is what we call animals and tables and things that don't matter. I wasn't going to stay if they didn't want me. I walked right out of there, and nobody said anything to me.

I went to the front of the hospital and asked to use their phone, and I called up my friend, Anthony, and asked him to come get me. He picked me up in his car, and he drove me across town to another hospital. He was a really big fella, and he said not to worry.

We went to the ER, and he says to the receptionist, "My friend here hurt her leg, and I want you to be real nice to her."

They took me to the back room, and they asked me the same questions again. When I told them why I don't have periods, Anthony said, "Now, you don't treat her any different."

Every one of the nurses there was really nice to me. A few minutes later, they took me to some dark room and they X-rayed my leg. A little while after that, the doctor came in and showed me the X-ray, and you know what happened? It was broken in three places.

WENDY

Five or six years ago I had already started transitioning. I was read as female pretty frequently. I wanted to see the doctor because I had slipped off a curb while walking, and I was pretty sure I had broken my ankle. I told the doctor what had happened, and as is routine, he asked what medications I was taking. I told him I was on estrogen, blah, blah, blah. At that point, I had been taking estrogen for years, and of course, it's not big news to me that I'm trans. The conversation shifted very quickly to whether or not I had undergone genital reconstruction. I'm not a doctor, but I'm reasonably certain that whether or not I have a vagina has nothing to do with how I broke my ankle.

ERIK

My worst experience with the health system happened when I was an undergrad. I haven't told many people about this. It's been over two years now, but every time I think about it I just get so riled up. I was a junior in college, and at this point, I'd been taking testosterone for over a year. My voice was low, I had some facial hair, my breasts were really small, and I'd usually bind them—so no one ever suspected that I was anything but male. Anyway, I was visiting a guy I knew in high school, and I thought he was okay with the trans thing, but . . . well, to put it bluntly, things turned bad, and he ended up sexually assaulting me . . . Whatever. It is what it is.

So, my partner took me to the walk-in clinic, and when we got there he told the receptionist what had happened, and a little while later they called me into an exam room. The doctor comes in, and my partner tells her what happened. She asks me if I want an exam, and I say no; I couldn't stand the thought of anyone else touching me just then. She shrugged and told me there was nothing more she could do for me, and she just walked out of the room. I was so embarrassed. I didn't know what I was supposed to do, so we left. About the time we get to the parking lot I start to get upset. They didn't give me a Z-Pak, and they didn't ask me if I wanted Plan B, and they didn't offer to call a victim advocate. I don't know why it took me as long as the parking lot to think of this, but I turned around and went back in.

I go up to the receptionist and tell her I want to be seen. *Again.* Immediately, one of the nurses takes me into a room, and I tell her that the first doctor didn't really help me. So she gives me some sort of antiviral shot in the hip, and she hands me an antibiotic cocktail to drink when I get home. Then she hands one to my partner and tells him in a really snide way that he should probably drink one too. I couldn't believe it.

So I leave the exam room, and I walk over to the clinic supervisor's office and knock on the door. She lets me into her office, and I tell her that the first doctor was incredibly hostile and sent me away without helping and that the second nurse was really rude. She asked me why I didn't just go to my regular doctor. I told her that my doctor was full and that it didn't matter who I saw; I expected to be treated with a little human decency. She said, "Well, we'll try to do better next time."

It was like a ton of bricks. "Next time? Why would there be a next time?"

She turned her computer screen so I could see it and said, "It says in your chart that this isn't the first time you've had this happen. I expect you'll be back soon."

I didn't know what to say. My partner didn't either. We just sat there. I was in total shock . . . I mean, it was true, that was the second time in my life I'd been raped. It was in my file 'cause I'd been seen for depression after the first time. But I know that if I had gone into their office as a woman, they would have never treated me like that.

I left the supervisor's office. I wasn't going to stay there and have her belittle me. I mean, I'd just been raped, you know? I walked back through the waiting room to the exit and just before I reached the door I collapsed. I just started crying hysterically. I've never felt so lost or hurt. What she said to me was so much worse than what he did to me . . . I just sat on the floor crying. I couldn't breathe. It was the first and only time I'd ever had a panic attack. The supervisor came out and told me to get up. Then she grabbed my arm and tried to yank me to my feet. I told her not to touch me, I know I probably yelled it, and she went back into her office. My partner helped me up and took me to the car. He was so sweet. He didn't know what to do either, so he drove me to the counseling center. I was still crying hysterically when we got there.

The counselor I saw when I came out as trans called us into her office immediately. It was the end of the day, and she was just about to leave. She picked up the phone and called her husband and told him that he needed to pick up their son from day care. Then she called the ER to see who the attending was. She drove us to the ER and stayed there the entire time. She said, "Nobody will treat you like that if I'm there," and she was right. Everyone was really nice and helpful. She was a lifesaver. I don't know what I'd have done if she hadn't been such a great advocate for me.

A few weeks after, I got a letter in the mail from the walk-in clinic supervisor. It said that they would not tolerate my behavior and that I had thirty days to pick up my file. They banned me from going back. I told my counselor about it, and she was furious. She called them and told them any poor behavior on my part was a symptom of their misconduct.

CATHERINE

There are a number of things I've noticed working at a large hospital. We are great with confidentiality, but we are terrible with privacy. In the emergency department, there is a desk at the front of the room. There are usually one or two somewhat elderly and reasonably deaf ladies at the desk. You have to very clearly enunciate what your problem is. Directly behind them is a corner of the room, and I swear it was built for acoustical reflection. If the women behind the desk can hear you, so can everyone in the waiting room.

How do you get seen? When a deep voice over the phone says, "I need a Pap smear," the line is going to go dead. They'll think it's a prank. You can be a wonderful provider, the best provider in the world, but if the patient can't get to you, what good is that? The office staff is so important. You need receptionists and secretaries and nurses who can maintain confidentiality, can maintain privacy, who are compassionate and know how to work with trans people.

Trans people are really intuitive, and we can tell the difference between when you call us by the wrong pronouns by mistake and when you do it on purpose. We know. We can see the look in your eyes. We know how we're being touched. We can tell whether or not you care as a physician.

The results of my surgeries came out great: I can get through cursory pelvic examination, and my doctors would never know I'm trans. I can go to any doctor and know that I will never have a problem. If I don't tell them that I'm trans, they'll never know. I can go to the emergency department and be treated for a broken arm, for a rash, even for a gynecological issue, and I have no problems doing it the day that symptoms appear. If I were a trans man, and I were having a gynecological issue, I might think, "I don't really want to go to the emergency department because they're not going to know how to treat me. Let's see, it's Friday? I'll just wait till Monday, and then maybe I'll go to my primary care physician."

At that point, it's already been three days. There could be a major issue and they haven't gone to see a doctor because they're afraid they're going to be discriminated against. It happens. It happens all the time, and this is why trans folk don't get the care that they need. We wait until we are forced into it, because we're too afraid to go.

Individuals with intersectional identities often experience additional medical gatekeeping.

VICKY

I've had cross-gender feelings my entire life, but I've only had the vocabulary to express my identity for the past few years. I knew I wanted to transition, but when I brought it up with my counselor, my other mental-health issues came into play. I put myself in a vulnerable state by telling my counselor that I was transgender and intended on transitioning. She replied, "But you have schizoaffective disorder. How can you possibly know that you're trans? How could you possibly know what's real about your identity?"

DIANE

There aren't a lot of studies on how bigger people respond to anesthesia. There is a lot of fear of people dying during surgical procedures, and for that reason, as a matter of course, you'll be told you need to lose a certain amount of weight before you have a procedure done. I was told that I should exercise to lose weight, but exercising one day usually means that I can't get out of bed for the next two and I actually gain more weight.

It's very common, and it's devastating for fat people who are waiting for health care all the time. Health issues are blamed on our body size, partly because it's the only thing that's seen as liminal, that's changeable. Unfortunately, most of the time, weight loss is not something that's permanent or safe or sustainable. For me, my weight and the medical issues it's caused intersects so much with my disability, with my trans identity, with my identity as a person of color. Not only am I seen as being suspect; my weight causes me to be seen as particularly lazy.

HILLARY

Being a fat woman, my mental-health problems get taken quite un-seriously, and that's a very big problem. "You're depressed? Lose weight. You're deaf? Lose weight! You're autistic? Lose weight!"

Yeah, thanks, that's helpful. There is a lot of medical gatekeeping around weight, and even more so for trans people. I have vaginoplasty coming up in a few months, and I have to lose x number of pounds before then, because Lord knows we can't let the fatties through the system.

I have spoken to more than one surgeon in this community who explained to me that people with a large body mass index don't get good results, which means that they don't have good pictures to put on their website. My response? Learn to get good results on bodies that are fat.

There are many trans people who self-identify as fat who are unsurprisingly frustrated with the medical gatekeeping surrounding weight and surgery. Surgeons are often likewise frustrated when they cannot provide gender-confirming surgeries to overweight patients but are concerned with the higher risks of complications and wound healing. However, these gaps can sometimes be bridged by trans folk who also work in health care, as they can provide really insightful recommendations for how to make medical settings more trans friendly.

DIANE

As a former health-care provider, I was in a position to speak up if I heard medical discrimination. I corrected people if I heard them use the wrong pronouns for a patient. We had a nurse who had been working with trans patients for twenty years, and I would still correct her on pronouns if she got them wrong. She would correct me if I made mistakes as well. Sometimes it's not clear in which direction a person is transitioning, and it's okay to ask them for their preferred pronouns. Most of the time, they will be really grateful that you asked instead of just assumed. It doesn't matter who I'm treating, my role as a health-care provider was to be an advocate for patients. If I wasn't doing that, I wasn't doing my job.

SUPRIYA

As a physician, it can be difficult to switch pronouns or names for a patient that I've been seeing for ten years. Sometimes I stumble, and I really kick myself for it because I remember how terrible it made me feel when someone used the wrong pronouns for me early in my transition. The way I look at it is that patients change their names all the time. We have a formal process for women to change their names through our office after they get married, and we're very careful about making sure they've updated their name through their insurance company before we begin the billing process. Doctors' offices need to show that same courtesy to transgender patients. After all, transitioning is at least as important as getting married.

TAYLOR

I spent a year working on my master's degree at the University of Adelaide in Australia. While I was there, I got to see the doctor for free. The physicians always seemed more blasé about my status as a trans person. When I told them I was trans, it didn't affect how they treated me. In the States you always get the same invasive questions: When was your last period? Why don't you have periods? Why don't you have a uterus? Fuck, I'm here for a cold. Is this really relevant?

Australian doctors just seemed much more cool about it. I even got to have little time-release hormone capsule implanted into my hip for free. The surgery took place in-office. They numbed my hip with a local anesthetic, made a small incision, and placed the implant inside. I only had to have two stitches. The entire procedure lasted less than five minutes. The implant was amazing. I'd get to wake up, I wouldn't have to take a pill; I wouldn't have to worry about anything. It was brilliant. Unfortunately, I have no idea why, but you can't actually get these implants in the U.S. Even if they were available, insurance wouldn't cover it.

KURTIS

I currently have the best medical care I've ever received. My doctor is brilliant, and he is incredibly compassionate. He's an endocrinologist, and he basically treats all of the trans folk in the area. He works at the public medical center and runs the student health center as well. I have no idea how he finds time to do everything.

One of the reasons that he is such an amazing advocate is because he lets trans folk speak for themselves. He provides trainings to his fourth-year advanced medical students each year and asks a panel of transgender patients to tell them stories about health care. I've sat on panels that he's arranged to train endocrinology section nurses, the billing and reception staff at the hospital, various groups of medical students, and even a licensed practitioner conference. My doctor will get up, give a short speech about the medical science of transitioning, and open the floor for four or five of his trans patients to tell our stories.

Unlike all of my prior physicians, he didn't say, "Take your clothes off so I can see if I actually want to work with you." Instead he said,

"How are you? How long have you been on hormones? Okay, have you had any problems? No? Great. If you have any problems, feel free to talk to me."

Before the exam I asked if I'd need to get undressed. He said, "I'm never going to make you take your clothing off. Because I'm your doctor I have to suggest that you get a yearly pelvic exam, but I'm not going to force you to because I know that's really uncomfortable for most trans patients." That's the most respectful a doctor has been to me. With all the terrible treatment I've received over the years, I lived in fear of going to the doctor. Finally meeting a doctor that was respectful toward me has been incredible. It gives me hope for the future.

We need more compassionate doctors like this. Yes, there will always be a handful of medical professionals who are purposefully discriminatory, but I think overall, the majority of them just haven't had much exposure to trans folk. The more we can increase their level of understanding, the better the treatment we're going to get. This work is invaluable, and I'm so glad to know that for every physician who refuses to treat a trans patient, there is another one out there batting for us.

It's So Damn Hard to Get a Job

FELIPE

In Alaska you can still lose your job or be evicted for being gay, much less trans. I am protected through my company, which is one of the reasons I picked them. All these companies are playing the resources game, because there aren't enough experienced and educated individuals in this area. Oftentimes another company will try to recruit me, but because they don't have policies for LGBT folks in place, I won't even look at them. It gets really hard to explain why without outing myself. I'm protected right now, and I will not lose my job over being trans. If I moved to another company, I could. I feel some amount of comfort knowing that I have some protection in place. At the same time, my roommate and I could all get evicted at any point for being gay, so working in Alaska still has its downsides.

CATHERINE

When I got my job at the university medical center, I had to come out to my potential boss in the beginning of the hiring process. I was making one more try to get back into orthopedics. I finally figured out that someone had been torpedoing my references. Previously, I had worked for Newark Orthopedics. I didn't know exactly who it was coming from, but I knew somebody there was giving me a bad reference. They told me at Princeton that I look great on paper, but they wanted to check my references before they interviewed me. I had to e-mail back and say, "Let me tell you about an issue with my references. Somebody at Newark Orthopedics is torpedoing my references and here's why."

I was surprised to get an e-mail back that said, "I congratulate you for taking such a major step in your life. You look great on paper. Let's meet for breakfast."

We met for breakfast, and I knew I was being judged on whether or not I passed. If I didn't, I wouldn't get a job. Luckily for me, the interview went off without a hitch, and I was hired a few weeks later.

JUANITA

I've never turned tricks,[3] but a lot of my friends end up doing it because it's so damn hard to get a job. No one wants to hire someone who they think looks like a freak. Well, if you hired me I'd have more money for surgery and then I wouldn't look like a freak. [laughs]

Juanita's statement is a very poignant commentary on the intersection of socioeconomic status and the ability of trans folk to access desired medical procedures, which can lead to being read more consistently as the gender with which one identifies.

---

3. Slang for engaging in sex work.

I was living and working as a mechanic in Montgomery, Alabama. I knew I wouldn't be able to transition in Alabama, and I knew I'd lose my job in the process if I tried. I floated the idea of transitioning by my supervisor once, and the response was not good. He told me that he wouldn't let freaks work in his garage, and shortly thereafter all of the other employees started to become increasingly hostile toward me. I quit a few weeks later.

I knew that there were a lot of surgeons in Massachusetts, so I hopped in my car and drove to Boston. I had nothing left for me in Alabama. My parents kicked me out of the house when I was fourteen for being a dyke, so I had no family ties.

My first few years in Boston were pretty rough. I needed to get a job before I could start my transition, but there aren't a lot of garages that want to hire a female mechanic. I also knew that as soon as my transition got into the swing, I would have to quit and try to find another garage where no one knew me. It was a nightmare.

I started taking testosterone, and after a few months my voice had lowered substantially. Some customers still called me she, but most of them referred to me as a guy. Since I was being seen as male more often than female, I figured it was time to change my name. A month later, I was put on suspension at work. Too many of the other guys complained about working with me, so they were looking for any reason to fire me. I quit before they had the opportunity.

I work at a different garage now. When I applied for the job, I said that I was male on the application form. At this point, I pass really well, so they don't know the difference. I'm stealth at work, but I have to be really careful that no one ever finds out that I'm not fully a guy, or else I'll be looking for work again.

Intersectional Identities Equal
Intersectional Discrimination

For those who experience multiple axes of oppression, discrimination is often more prevalent and overt.

GREG

One of the things that really pisses me off is, when I'm on the street, people will assume that just because there's something wrong downstairs that there's something wrong upstairs. It happens when I'm in my wheelchair, as well as when I use crutches. I was crossing the street last week, and a woman came up to me, bent right down so her face was a few inches away from me, and said, "Are you lost?"

When I told her I knew perfectly well where I was, she asked if she could call someone for me. She talked to me like I was three years old. Last I checked, I had a beard, so she knew I wasn't young; she just assumed I was special needs and that I shouldn't be out roaming the town by myself. I don't even want to leave the house some days because I don't want to have to face that ridicule, not all the time. If I have a snappy retort, they get pissed off at me. Sometimes I really just don't want to leave the house, which is bad for my mobility, because then I'm just sedentary and that's a nasty set of circumstances. I shouldn't have to hang a sign around my neck that says, "Don't treat me like a child."

ZACH

People give my cane terrible looks. They assume that because I'm young I must be healthy, and I must not need a cane. I get looks from older people on the bus, and I just get the feeling that they assume I'm "faking" my disability in order to get government assistance or something. Newsflash, I'm not on disability or any other assistance.

It's funny because certain medical instruments are seen for certain people or conditions. Walkers are unisex, but canes are for older men. Some people will look at me, then look away if they notice that I saw them staring. It's human nature to be curious, so ask me questions instead of just assuming what must be wrong with me. I'm friendly.

Occasionally, people will ask me why I use a cane. I tell them that

I have fibromyalgia and that I need the cane to walk. What would their response be if I had said I hurt my ankle? Is one reason more legitimate than the other?

I face enough harassment as a trans person that I feel like when I add my cane to it I'm just a walking freakish billboard. I guess intersectional identities equal intersectional discrimination. If I'm going to be somewhere I know I'll be safe, I'll leave the cane at home; that would be anywhere where I'm relatively certain someone will help me up. I know I'll only have to lie there for an hour or something if I fall and can't get up. [*laughs*]

Bias, suspicion, and increasingly invasive security protocols can mean that acts as simple as traveling can be nightmarish for transgender individuals.

SUPRIYA

The last time I visited my family in India I had a layover in Turkey. I was stopped in the airport no fewer than six times. Six times I was asked to remove my shoes or other parts of my clothing. Six times I was asked a series of invasive questions about my gender, about my nationality, and about my green card. Six times my bag was unceremoniously searched.

Before I left the U.S., I was standing in line for coffee prior to my flight, and an officer pulled me out of the queue and submitted me to hours of questioning. I was viewed as a suspicious person. I don't think there was anything brow-raising about my drink order; I suspect that my real crime was flying while brown.

Of course, once they took me into a back room, they asked to see all of my documents. My passport, green card, and other forms of ID were all obtained at different times. In some of the pictures I look more masculine, and in some I look more feminine. Even though all of my IDs say "female" and say my correct name, I received each one at a different point in transition, so they do not necessarily reflect me exactly as I look now. A simple interrogation led to hours of investigation while I explained over and over again why my ID pictures were inconsistent. They finally let me leave, but I had missed my flight.

DAKOTA

The last time I flew I said I didn't want to go through the body scanner. If you don't go through the scanner the Travel Safety Administration is supposed to have an officer of the same gender pat you down. It took the TSA a while to decide which officer should perform my pat down. I didn't get involved in the conversation and instead let them decide. Honestly, I didn't really care; there wasn't one officer or another that would have made me feel more comfortable. They ended up making the decision for me, and I think their choice was based on my voice because they selected a female officer to pat me down.

The Absurd Rules of Respectability Politics

Many trans folk come to expect discrimination from the outside world, but bias is also a prevalent problem in many LGBTQI communities. Some people focus on ensuring that LGBTQI communities appear respectable to outsiders as a tactic for promoting mainstream issues such as marriage equality. Those who do not outwardly represent mainstream values and appearances are often ostracized.

ERIK

Queers get touchy about pride parades. Everyone has a different idea of what gay pride should look like. I've walked in a few pride parades, which is always really fun. At one parade there were floats and pickup trucks full of fabulous drag queens; there were nudists on bicycles; [and] Dykes on Bikes, a lesbian motorcycle club, rode in the parade. We are such a hodgepodge mix of people, and I felt that this particular parade showed the diversity of the community. This community is an incredible medley.

I sat on a committee for planning a pride parade the following year. The planning meetings became incredibly hostile and divisive because some people thought the parade should reflect a certain sense of propriety. They didn't want anyone with dyed hair, tattoos, or piercings to march. They didn't want anyone who didn't "pass" to march. They definitely didn't want nudists. They only wanted mainstream, white gays and lesbians who didn't fulfill any stereotypes whatsoever. No short-haired lesbians, and definitely no trans people.

One of the organizers told me, "If the outside world thinks that we are a bunch of freaks who cannot exercise modesty, they are never going to accept us."

Bullshit! We *are* freaks, and we should be proud of that fact. That's what pride is about: accepting ourselves even when others do not. We are not a modest community and shouldn't pretend to be something we're not so that a bunch of pretentious breeders[4] will finally accept us. If cis and straight people don't want to include us, why are we trying to force them? I don't want to be invited to their tables. Let's get together with other freaks and make new tables. There are so many queers who don't want to focus on mainstream issues, and so many more who will never fit into the absurd rules of respectability politics. This is particularly true for trans folk.

After trying to reason with some of the other organizers, several of us quit the committee. We rallied all of the not-so-respectable queers and freaks and trans folk together and crashed the parade. We made our own "Freaks Float" and joined the end of the parade. The organizers were furious with us, but the crowd seemed to love it. In fact, ours was voted the best float in the parade.

In the United States, queer visibility has long been a tactic for social change. While there are many trans folk who remain stealth for personal or safety reasons, others desire to maintain a strong trans presence in the public eye, as a pathway to greater acceptance.

---

4. Pejorative term for cisgender, heterosexual people.

JUANITA

I found out I had HIV when I was twenty-three. I never figured out exactly how I got it. It could have been sex; it could have been needles. I'll never know for sure. I was in rehab when I found out. They suggest that everyone take an HIV test while they are there, and I wasn't super surprised when my test was positive, but still, it was life-changing news.

Until I found out that I had HIV, I was trying to get clean. When I found out that I was dying, I figured I might as well enjoy myself. I dropped out of rehab and walked right back into my old life. I don't want anyone else to get it from me, though, so I don't use needles now.

You would think that the gay community would be really accepting of people with HIV. Nope. They view you as tainted and dirty. There is such a fear of AIDS in the community that no one wants anything to do with me. Jesus, I'm not trying to get you to sleep with me; I just want to be your friend.

The trans community is better about it. Then again, nearly every trans woman I know has it! Well, not many of the white ones do, but the rest of us do.

ALEXANDER

I am asexual and poly. I find that the poly community doesn't really have a place for people who are ace spectrum.[5] The implication of polyamory seems to be that you're not only having sex but having sex with more than one person. A lot of us are trying to explain the difference between romantic attraction and sexual attraction. My partner and I have been together for five years. He is sexual; I am not. And yet he doesn't go outside of our relationship to have his sexual needs met, and neither of us go out of our relationship to have our emotional needs met. This is very hard to navigate, and even more difficult to explain to others.

---

5. Ace is slang for asexual. Asexuality is viewed as a spectrum of identities.

HILLARY

Sexuality and physicality is not just celebrated in the queer community; it's mandatory. You find this in queer Deaf space, in queer disability space, and in queer autistic space. Outside of queer space, people assume that if you have a disability or you are deaf, that you must be asexual. It's the inaccurate stereotype that disabled people don't have sex lives.

But in queer disabled spaces, there is a push to prove that we do have sex lives and that we are still sexual beings. When I came out to one of my disabled friends as asexual, she groaned and said, "If you tell people that, they'll think we're all asexual and some of us still want to get laid. You're not doing the community any favors."

Disabled people don't want you to speak out about your experiences because they say you are fulfilling a stereotype, and that's bad for the community. I told my friend, "I'm sorry that you are negatively affected by this stereotype, but I am queer, disabled, and still asexual. I'm not going to lie about who I am because you're worried about the community's image."

JAIME

I've gotten the most grief from old-school lesbians who want to police my gender. There is a woman I work with, in her fifties, who reads me as a lesbian because of how I dress. I would often skate around pronouns when talking about my partner—I would say my significant other or "them"—and never actually specify who my partner was. She and I had a work relationship only and never really talked about our personal lives.

One day before a meeting I was talking to a different coworker about a condo my partner and I were looking at and how fantastic our new spice rack was and how much he loved it. The other woman's head did a 360. She said, "What did you say?"

So I repeated, "He. Chris. Loved the spice rack. He loves cooking; he's in the kitchen all the time."

She stumbled all over herself. "I'm really sorry about interrupting you—but I always assumed—and the way you dress."

I said, "Yeah, I get that a lot."

She pursed her lips and said, "The way you dress indicates to other people about who you are. You shouldn't be dressing that way if you don't identify."

I had been considering coming out to her as trans, but I realized this was apparently not a safe thing to do. I talked to my boss about it, and talked it through with quite a few other friends, and finally I sat down with this woman and said, "Do you remember when this happened? Do you remember what you said? Let me repeat it for you. It was gender policing, and it made me feel really uncomfortable."

She said, "I'm sorry, please call me on it if I do it again. I want to be an ally."

LUIS

There have been a number of major colleges and universities in the news over the past year for failing to report instances of hate crimes and sexual assault. According to the Clery Act, colleges are supposed to respond to reports of violence on campus in a certain way. Many colleges fail to do this, and students have held some pretty major protests at places like UNC [University of North Carolina at Chapel Hill], Occidental, Dartmouth, and Swarthmore. A delegation of students from each of these colleges and a few others met in New York to hold a press conference.

Before we got there, the delegation from our campus was told that the press conference was going to be intersectional. We were going to talk about racism, transphobia, homophobia, sexual assault, and everything else surrounding the culture of hostility on college campuses. Our group was made up primarily of queer folk and people of color. The other colleges sent mostly white, cisgender, heterosexual women. It was like a sorority: short skirts, makeup, and long, blonde hair. If any of them were queer, they wouldn't get called a dyke or a fag on the street. My partner Gui and I were the only trans men.

The day before the press conference, a battle started over what we should talk about. Was it sexual assault only? Gui argued that if we broadened the discussion to the culture of hostility happening on our campuses, it would cover everything that we were there to address. We had been told that the conference would be egalitarian and student run, and everyone would have a chance to speak. However, the agenda became just sexual assault: they didn't want to talk about racism or homophobia. They said, "We have to do this because sex sells."

No! We need to talk about everything because we are so rarely given such an amazing platform to talk about these really important issues that impact our campus just as much, if not more, than sexual assault.

We were then each asked to write statements of what we were going to say on camera. There was a very high-profile, white lawyer who had decided to help us with the press conference. All of the students were very much enamored by her, and they ended up letting her steer the shape of the conference. She said that everyone had to send her their statements and she would edit them and give them back, which is not what we wanted to do. We said, "No, we speak for ourselves — that's a very important distinction."

We got tired of arguing with her, so we eventually capitulated and just gave her our statements to look over. I was really frustrated with how the lawyer was trying to take over the press conference and how the other women were narrowing the focus of the event. They said that we couldn't talk about racism and homophobia at the press conference because saying racism and homophobia exist is like saying the sky is blue. Isn't saying sexual assault exists like saying the sky is blue? Sexual assault is everywhere! I was told that I needed to accept the girls who might be racists and who might not be allies if they were willing to come out about their sexual assaults. I stayed really quiet and tried to focus on the goal at hand.

Not long after that, a few of the girls from another college came up to Gui and I and said, "The coalition has decided that you are not allowed to speak at the press conference and that you are not allowed to attend."

From there it just blew up. We were like, "What!? Are you crazy? Is this because we want to emphasize intersectionality? What are you talking about?"

Yelling started to occur. We were told that our masculinity was triggering. This may have been okay, except for the fact that there were cismale reporters in the room. We were kicked out because our masculinity was too much for them to deal with. When we weren't in the room, they mocked our posture. They were mocking the way we stood, mocking our identities as trans men, and mocking us culturally as Latinos.

When Gui and I mentioned that they were kicking out the only two trans men of color, one of the girls came an inch from my face and yelled, "I'm queer too!"

She was trying to say that because she was queer too, she wasn't being transphobic. You can be queer and still be transphobic. She's a ciswoman who is married to a cisman. She has all of the privilege of being married. Of course she could be queer, but she was ignoring how much privilege she had. As we were leaving, she yelled, "You don't know what real violation is!"

She invalidated my experience as a rape survivor. And she implied that the only type of "real" violation is rape. Another one of the girls yelled, "Go destroy the movement! Go destroy the movement, ladies!"

So obviously, in her mind, she didn't view us as men. Yet they kicked us out because they found our masculinity triggering. You can't have it both ways.

KURTIS

My undergrad college had a Gay-Straight Alliance [GSA], and I served as their event programmer for a few terms. The president of the group was one of my best friends, and this created a really awkward situation. I felt like I couldn't call her out when she did something transphobic because I didn't want to hurt our friendship.

The GSA wasn't particularly versed on trans issues. They started in the nineties, and there wasn't a lot of trans consciousness at the time. Fifteen years later, they were still holding the same events with no real realization that many of these events weren't accessible to the growing number of trans folks on campus. At one of our meetings, my friend said we were going to throw a pool party. I mentioned that it wasn't really a great inclusive option for most trans people. She turned to me and said, "Well, we're all queer so trans people can just wear whatever they want to the pool and it will be fine."

I started ranting in my head: "Really? It will be fine. If I take my shirt off and my tits are hanging out, that will be fine? If a pre-op trans woman has half a testicle hanging out of her swimsuit, that'll be fine? If the trans guys who have had top surgery take off their shirts, you're telling me no one is going to gawk at their scars?"

I didn't say this out loud because I didn't think the middle of a meeting was an okay place to call her out. When I tried to bring up the fact that some of our other events weren't welcoming to trans folk, she told me, "Well there are only like two of you, so does it really matter?"

Yes. It matters. It always matters. There are only a few of us who come to meetings because the rest of the campus trans population knows that the GSA is exclusionary and they don't want to subject themselves to that. I knew if I pressed the issue further we would get nowhere and we would end up damaging our friendship. When you're trans, you're not allowed to talk about trans issues, in the same way that President Obama isn't allowed to talk about black issues. It's hard to push back when you're the one being marginalized.

Accidental Activists

One of the most remarkable trends I found when collecting interviews was a tendency toward activism. Nearly every individual whose voice is featured in this project engages in activism on a regular basis. Even Felipe, who is incredibly stealth, finds ways to give back to his community. Just like their stories of transition, there is no single trajectory of how the interviewees came to be activists or how they define activism.

GREG

My activism predates my transition. I was already active in education through a series of speakers' bureaus and outreach events on my campus. We had very few trans folk on our panels, so I started making trans issues a talking point. Little did I realize that I was becoming a bastion for a cause that I would get to know even more intimately over the coming years.

I feel that a lot of trans folk become activists, not because they necessarily want to, but because there is a certain amount of need. You can't change the gender marker on your driver's license? You can't find a doctor willing to treat you? You can't find a safe restroom? No one else is going to take care of these issues, because their lives aren't affected by them each and every day. As you deal with prejudice on a daily basis, you start picking and choosing which battles are the most important to you and then you start educating the people around you. Even if they never intended for it to happen, I believe most trans people become accidental activists.

When I was in college, there were two trans men on campus who got the shit kicked out of them for being queer. Everybody overlooked it. Campus administration handled it very poorly: when we brought up the fact that there had been three attacks on queer students in the past five days, they told us that we should all try to be less overtly gay. When we said that we weren't going to stop being queer, they stopped talking to us at all.

Up until that point, I had a highly romanticized idea of what activism looked like. To me there were two ways to be an activist: you could take part in a major protest, like the WTO [World Trade Organization] protests in Seattle in the late nineties, or you could sit in an office and write letters as a form of lobbying. There were these two big extremes in my head, and I didn't really like the idea of having the shit kicked out of me by cops. I've been intimidated by cops enough in my life that this form of activism hadn't ever appealed to me. Yet, all of a sudden, there were queers on our campus who were being harassed. As the president of the LGBTQ student club, there were threats on my life. I had to lay all of my fears aside and do something.

When the administration made no attempt to do anything about the series of antiqueer attacks that happened on campus, we got loud. There were a lot of rallies and a lot of ruckus making on this rural, conservative campus. We yelled until someone would listen. The media listened first, which finally got the administration to listen. The local LGBTQ community started protesting, and we were featured on international news before the campus administration even made a formal statement. It felt like we were holding their hands a lot of the time. I think most of the administrators wanted to make the campus safer, but they were so freaked out by change and so worried about how they would look in the eyes of alumni. However, addressing the hate crimes when they happened would have been better than trying to sweep them under the rug and pretending they didn't happen at all.

I was responsible, in part, for organizing a rally against the hate speech and hate crimes that had happened on campus. We had a huge turnout. We sent formal invitations to all of the main campus administrators inviting them to come and listen to the issues that students were having on their campus. Since they wouldn't talk to us directly, we were having these conversations in a public forum. Having administrators show up to our rally would at least be a step in the right direction, as the university was getting tons of bad publicity by this point. We held the rally as a forum for students to speak out about their experiences with homophobia and transphobia on campus, and we explicitly said that faculty and administrators were not allowed to speak at the rally. After a while, the president of the university came up and tried to make a statement. I got to hold onto the microphone and tell him no; this was a forum for students, and this was his chance to listen. For once, it was not his turn to talk. If he wanted to make a statement, he could do so later through one of the many channels that his title as president of the university afforded him. I still have a picture that somebody took of me pulling the microphone away from him and shaking my head posted on my refrigerator.

There was certainly plenty of homophobia and transphobia among the administrators, but I believe that many of them wanted to do the right thing; they just didn't know how. It fell on the shoulders of all of the LGBTQ students and staff to come up with solutions, with only mixed support from administration. This was hardly an isolated incident: LGBTQ folks take on the role of activist or educator because they are constantly tread on. We get tired of discrimination and harassment and then we do something about it.

SETH

I went to my first Dyke March and discovered the Lesbian Avengers had organized it. After I learned more about the Lesbian Avengers as a direct-action, do-it-yourself organizing group, I decided to start a branch in Northampton. I was shocked that one didn't already exist there since there were so many lesbians at Smith College. We met at my apartment and did fun shit like make up lesbian Christmas carols to sing on the street. Another time we went to a mall in one of the surrounding towns and gave out Hershey's Kisses with the words "You've been kissed by a lesbian" on the tag. Twenty years ago, it was a very homophobic area. People threw the kisses back at us and told us we were sick, disgusting, and perverted, and that we shouldn't be allowed to have children.

Working with the Lesbian Avengers was my first taste of having political community. It became super important to me, because before that I had been really isolated. I didn't have a queer consciousness; I didn't know such a thing existed. To go from seeing myself as a totally isolated, abnormal, crazy person to being a part of identity-based political community was huge.

JUANITA

I never saw the point of activism. I thought it was just a bunch of angry people yelling about how unfair life is, and I figured it wouldn't change anything, so why bother. After I was diagnosed with HIV, I started going to an AIDS support group. I didn't know much about HIV, or what medications I needed to be taking, or how long I was going to live. I still thought that people got AIDS and died right away. When I started going to these support groups, I met people who had been diagnosed ten years ago who were still walking around just fine! I thought, "Damn! Maybe I'm better off than I thought."

At the first few meetings I stayed real quiet. I didn't know what to say, and I was really depressed. The next time the group met up, I started asking all sorts of questions. One of the other trans women pulled me aside and said, "Mamí, you need to learn your history."

She told me that I should start volunteering with ACT UP.[1] I can't remember everything that they've done, but basically ACT UP

---

1. AIDS Coalition to Unleash Power.

started with a group of people in New York City in the 1980s. AIDS was everywhere, and gay men were dying left and right, but the government wasn't doing much about it. There was only one medication that people living with AIDS could take, and it was a hell of an expense, so ACT UP started protesting on Wall Street and places like that. Since then, ACT UP has started doing a lot of other things like handing out safer-sex kits and running awareness campaigns. They still do a lot of work to try to make HIV meds cheaper, and they have branches in different places.

We Have to Fight Because
No One Else Is Going To

Activism is broad and varied. Sometimes activists stage large events or protests; other times activism can be as simple as mentoring a child in one's community.

SETH

The biggest action that I did wasn't one that I personally organized. In the summer of 2000, I went to Camp Trans,[2] which was organized by the Boston Lesbian Avengers and the Chicago Lesbian Avengers. Camp Trans existed at the time to get inclusion for MTF [male-to-female] trans women but was primarily made up of FTMs [female to males]. There was one outspoken, almost token, MTF named Stacey who was totally cool. The rest were these FTMs who were talking about how they weren't welcome on the land, which they totally were, so it was kind of odd. I understand that people now read about Camp Trans in their gender studies classes, and they use terms like "postmodernist dialectical blah, blah, blah." I was there staging the protest, and I don't even know what they're

---

2. A protest held outside of the Michigan Womyn's Music Festival to voice opposition to the festival's womyn-born-womyn policy. The enforcement of the policy often meant that trans women were not allowed to attend the festival and would be escorted from the grounds if they were discovered to be trans.

talking about. There's clearly a divide between academics and the organizers.

Two of the organizers, Stacey and Simon, had created a zine[3] that supported trans inclusion in the festival. Lynnee Breedlove was also in the festival on stage as the lead singer of Tribe 8. The members of Sister Spit were also speaking on stage about trans inclusion. Those people later got bashed for going into the festival.

A bunch of the other Lesbian Avengers and I staged a protest in the festival. At the time, we didn't have the word genderqueer yet, so we were using terms like nonbinary gender. I was arguing to the organizers that you can't draw a line defining who is male and who is female because some people aren't either one, or are right in between, or are outside of those categories altogether. I think it was one of the Michfest organizers who called us up one by one and asked us to share how we identified. The people who identified themselves as transsexual had to leave; the people who identified as transgender didn't have to leave. I had identified as transgender, but I thought the line she drew was so arbitrary that I chose to march out with the people who had been thrown out. As we marched out, women who were camping yelled derogatory things at us: "Get out, you don't belong here, go home!"

They cut off our armbands, and we went back to Camp Trans. Somebody gave me her armband so I could go back in and continue the dialogue, so I went back and helped Lynnee Breedlove organize a discussion group around trans inclusion.

CAMERON

I started working with the Trans Youth Equality Foundation (TYEF) in July of 2012. Prior to that, I was working full time for a legal research firm, and I hated it. I began looking for some kind of volunteer work that I could do to be happier and feel more fulfilled.

---

3. A low budget, small-scale, self-published booklet on a specific topic. Often zines are informative or political in nature and distributed free of charge, or as a fundraiser for nonprofit organizations.

I found an ad looking for an intern for a trans organization, so I responded and set up an interview with the director, Susan.

Susan started TYEF along with her husband. The administration is very centered around her family. Her son, Kyle, was born female and from a very young age started dressing as a boy. It became a personal struggle between their family and the school systems. They began moving around to find an accepting community. Susan had an art dealership and sort of stopped doing that to dedicate herself to this cause. She has really been the driving force behind the organization. When people call the number on the website, it goes to her cell phone. She's constantly on the phone with parents and kids.

About two days after I started, they held a big retreat for trans and gender-nonconforming kids. Suddenly, I went from not knowing any trans people in the area to meeting thirty of them all at once, all who were between the ages of thirteen and seventeen. I was very much thrown into the deep end. Whenever we have a retreat, I do everything from shuttling people around to doing ad-hoc counseling or crisis intervention. When we don't have retreats, I'm doing a lot of communication, editing podcasts, managing our Kickstarter, and creating a sex-ed zine. The organization is really based around the retreats, and we have several throughout the year. With these sorts of kids, you need a different organizational structure that's not so hardened and bureaucratic. One of the more difficult issues is gathering funding. We're starting to apply for more grants, but it's mostly just donations from parents at this point.

The kids are the best part of my job. They are so self-aware, and it comes very naturally to them. It's a group of kids who have parental support and have a lot of privilege but who also have problems and issues that are very serious.

KELLY

Since I transitioned when I was an adolescent, I've always been very involved in the youth movement. There are a lot of trans youth who are fighting for fair treatment in their middle and high schools.

For youth, usually the biggest issues are centered on bathrooms, sports, and extracurricular activities.

When a kid transitions in middle school or high school, or sometimes even as early as elementary school, which bathroom do they use? They should be allowed to use whichever bathroom matches their gender identity, but sometimes parents of other students or administrators freak out and decide that trans students should use the staff bathroom. There have been countless cases where trans or disabled students have been told that they can only use the staff bathroom, and this isolates them from the other kids. For trans students who may be stealth, this is a big red flag to their peers. Why do you get to use that bathroom? You're not disabled, so what's wrong with you? It's not a legitimate solution.

These same issues crop up in gym class. Which locker room do trans students use? What about if they try out for sports? Will they be allowed? These are the major issues that trans youth face in school, and now that I'm an adult, I work as an advocate for trans students. I go into a lot of the area schools and speak with administrators and parents to develop policies around working with transgender students.

DIANE

The bathroom issue is a major concern for trans folk, and it's a very intersectional issue. Many people with disabilities, intersex individuals, and transgender individuals need gender-neutral bathrooms. Using the restroom is a basic biological need, and being able to do so safely is a human right. About ten years ago a group of students at the University of California, Santa Barbara, started an organization called PISSAR that worked across this intersectionality. The name is an acronym that stands for "People In Search of Safe and Accessible Restrooms."

PISSAR created a questionnaire that people could fill out about each of the bathrooms on campus to determine whether that bathroom should be considered safe and accessible. The survey includes questions about the width of stall doors, whether or not the bathroom has grab bars for people in wheelchairs, whether the bathroom is gender neutral and has a working lock, and so on. Groups similar to PISSAR exist in various pockets of the country, and I volunteer with one such group. We've expanded and updated PISSAR's checklist, but the groundwork they did was wonderful. We're working on mapping bathrooms in several cities and creating maps of all of the safe, accessible public restrooms in town. We create maps listing all of the compliant bathrooms for the local LGBT centers, and then we submit all of the restrooms to an online database called Safe2Pee. They maintain a website where you can enter your zip code and find all of the gender-neutral or single-occupancy bathrooms near you.

HILLARY

My activism centers around reproductive rights, which intersects with trans rights and disability rights in more ways than one. I've volunteered for chapters of Planned Parenthood and Naral to fundraise and solicit donations. Once a month you can usually find me on a busy street or in a city park asking people for donations or getting them to sign up for pro-choice newsletters.

Last month an acquaintance of mine said, "If you're a trans woman, you don't have a womb, so reproductive rights can't possibly be of concern to you. Why are you such a flag waver for Planned Parenthood?"

Well, reproductive justice is about choice. I'm not just fighting for a woman's right to choose what happens to her body, I'm fighting for *everyone's* right to choose what happens to their bodies. Transgender people want to transition. Intersex people want autonomy over whether or not surgeries will be performed on them. Disabled individuals want to make their own health-care decisions to the best of their cognitive abilities. We *all* want to determine what happens to our bodies, and we should all be able to do that. Reproductive justice is a trans issue, an intersex issue, a disability issue, a women's issue, and a men's issue. It's a fight that affects everyone, and so we should all work toward the same goal: the right to choose.

While some focus on addressing issues on a community or personal level, others take state and federal legal or political actions to achieve their goals.

CATHERINE

In 2008, I was working with the group that would later become New Hampshire Freedom to Marry. It cracks me up that their initials are FTM because that means something very different in the trans community. We were trying to pass a marriage-equality measure in the state, which did later happen in 2009, but during the election cycle we got to meet Barack Obama.

It was early in the year, and he was speaking to a big LGBT caucus on his campaign trail. Mo, who was the organizer of New Hampshire FTM, arranged a smaller group meeting with Obama after the presentation. The snow was falling lightly, and it was freezing outside. His plane was on the runway, and they were spraying the de-icing stuff on it while he met with us. We were sitting around in this dingy room in the basement of the building, waiting. A few Secret Service agents came into the room and reminded us that we only had one hour. You could tell they wanted to leave because they stood in the corner tapping their feet impatiently and checking their watches.

Obama walked in, and the first thing out of Mo's mouth was, "We trusted Clinton, and he threw us under the bus. Why should we trust you?"

She was all business, and she's intimidating. Obama was great, though. He was very present in the room, he looked us in the eye, he shook our hands, and he remembered all of our names. Mo's questioning didn't get any easier from there, but he was incredibly calm under fire.

Marriage equality is a big issue, and it certainly affects trans folk. In 2012, marriage equality went to the ballot in Washington State. A marriage-equality bill was introduced, passed by both houses, and the governor signed it. It should have gone into effect as of May or June 2012. However, Preserve Marriage Washington, an anti-LGBT lobbying group, began collecting signatures in opposition of the marriage-equality bill. We knew we would encounter this type of backlash as soon as Governor Gregoire signed the bill, so we started our education campaign. We talked to people in front of grocery stores about the bill, what it meant for LGBT people in our state, and how it was important not to sign their petition sheets. We weren't successful in deterring people from signing the petitions, and the Preserve Marriage group got enough signatures to get a referendum on the ballot.

I worked with Washington United for Marriage to help people understand Referendum 74 and the importance of achieving marriage equality. We spoke to people outside of grocery stores, we went door to door, we held rallies, and we ran commercials. One of our Republican house representatives, Maureen Walsh, came out in support of gay marriage as her daughter is a lesbian. She took the stance that since, as a Republican, she doesn't support big government regulating the people's lives, she should likewise maintain that big government shouldn't regulate people's marriages. This was a really important moment because it gave many of the socially liberal Republicans in the state a valid argument for supporting marriage equality.

In 2012, there was an important election cycle for queer and trans folks. On Election Day, a bunch of us gathered in my apartment to watch the news. Our computers were up, and we were constantly refreshing our browsers to see if any new information was put online. We found out that President Obama was reelected first, so our spirits were pretty high. There are a lot of reasons that folks don't like Obama, and I don't know that I love the guy, but I know that Romney's stance on LGBT issues would have meant serious repercussions for those of us in the queer community, and especially for trans folk. We then heard that Maryland and Maine had passed their marriage-equality initiatives and that the proposed ban on same-sex marriage in Minnesota had been rejected. At each new announcement we became even giddier. People were jumping up and down screaming and hugging. There was so much love in that room.

Washington votes by mail, so it took a few additional days to completely confirm marijuana reform, marriage equality, and who won the governorship, which were our three biggest ballot issues. Washington is geographically and politically divided by a vertical line: east of the Cascades lies Seattle, which is known for being very liberal, and west of the Cascades is farming country, which is known for being quite conservative. When the ballot results for each county come in, the map of the state looks very red. There are really only a few counties that show up blue on voting maps. However, the overwhelming majority of people live in King County (where Seattle is located). You never know how an election is going to turn out until King County has finished counting their ballots.

Marriage equality passed 52 percent to 48 percent. Washington State had already had the most extensive domestic-partnership laws in the entire country because in 2009 the state had passed an "Everything but Marriage" law. It meant LGBT couples were entitled to all of the same rights and responsibilities as other married couples on a state level. The marriage-equality bill was nevertheless significant though. It meant that our voters, the people of Washington State, support LGBT marriage rights. In fact, 2012 was the first time that voters had upheld any referendum, law, or initiative in support of LGBT marriage. Washington, Maryland, Maine, and Minnesota were the four states that made history when their citizens voted pro-LGBT rights.

Marijuana was also decriminalized by ballot vote in Washington.

This is significant because it keeps a lot of people out of the prisons, out of the court systems, and in school. Previously, if you had a misdemeanor related to possession of marijuana, you were no longer eligible for financial aid to go to college. In Washington, you will no longer be charged for possessing small amounts of marijuana. This is important to the LGBT community because, especially among younger people, there is a high rate of marijuana use. It's partly a coping mechanism for dealing with the daily harassment, lack of familial support, and structural discrimination that we deal with as LGBT folks. I'm not saying that it's the best way to deal with these issues—just that the reality is a lot of queer folks smoke pot. Keeping them in school and out of jail is hugely important for the future of the community.

Because both marijuana reform and marriage equality passed in Washington at the same time, there were some pretty amusing jokes that came out of it. My favorite was the misappropriation of a line from Leviticus: "If a man lies with another man, as with a woman, they should both be stoned." [laughs]

QUINN

Cruising is a part of queer culture and has been for ages. Basically, cruising is when you go out and look to have sex with a stranger in a public or semipublic place. There is a long history of gays and bathhouses that fit into this culture. It's dangerous, of course, and probably contributed quite a bit to the rise of HIV during the 1980s, but it's still a prevalent activity that a lot of queer people take part in.

Along with this culture of promiscuity, there is still this 1960s tendency toward drug experimentation. I think a lot of straight people woke up from the haze of the sixties and decided to clean up their acts, settle down, and have families. At that time, blending into mainstream society wasn't an option for most queer people, so we just kept on having sex and experimenting with drugs. Sure, there are some who are focused on normative goals like marriage equality, but there are others who argue that free love and promiscuity is an important aspect of our culture and we shouldn't trade it in for monogamy and estate rights. The latter group tends to consist of people who are also fighting for drug reform.

There are high rates of drug use in the queer community. That fact is undeniable. Therefore, drug reform is a queer issue. We can either continue this war and drugs and say that the people who smoke pot or snort coke are terrible miscreants who deserve to be locked away in prison, which costs taxpayers tons of money, or we can recognize that marijuana does less harm to the body than alcohol and that people using harder drugs need rehab rather than prison. If we really want people to stop being addicts, locking them up where they are subject to rape and abuse isn't the answer. We need to decriminalize drugs and focus on creating better rehab programs and methadone clinics. We're not doing addicts any good by sending them to prison, and we're wasting time and resources by locking up a bunch of college kids who occasionally smoke marijuana.

I was involved in the movement to decriminalize marijuana possession in Portland, Maine. Maine can be pretty conservative at times, but Portland is a mecca of liberal queers. There is a lot of homelessness and a high rate of drug use in Portland, and it doesn't make sense to imprison college kids and homeless folks. We knew that Portlanders would approve sensible marijuana legislation, so we petitioned to get marijuana decriminalization on the ballet. I worked with the Portland Green Independent Committee to gather signatures of people who supported the ordinance. We had over 2,500 signatures by the time we gave the proposal to the city council.

As we waited for the ballot results to come in, we held a party with a reggae band and a belly dancer in true stoner fashion. Portlanders approved the measure by nearly 70 percent. It is now legal for adults twenty-one and over to have up to 2.5 ounces of marijuana. They can't smoke in public, [and] they can't sell it to children, but they can use it responsibly in the privacy of their own homes.

Trans people are arrested frequently. It's not necessarily that we participate in more crime than others, just that we look more suspicious. There's something disconcerting about someone who doesn't look strictly male or female. When you can't figure out someone's gender, it's off-putting, and it leaves us more vulnerable to police harassment, to stop-and-frisk laws, and to profiling.

We have statistics that prove that although white men are more likely to possess marijuana, African American men are more likely to have their cars searched for drugs when they are pulled over by the police. People of color are disproportionately subjected to stop-and-frisk laws. Just as people of color are targeted, so are transgender people. Transgender sex workers are more likely to be arrested for prostitution than cisgender sex workers. Trans women are more frequently assaulted and murdered than trans men. It goes down the line like that, so if you are a trans woman of color you are constantly in a really vulnerable place.

I've never used drugs, and I have no desire to start, but I am pro drug reform because I'm tired of this so-called war on drugs tearing apart my communities. There are too many poor black women and men in prison over a few ounces of marijuana. How does sending them to prison help them get clean? How does it help our families and our communities if their children are orphaned or they are no longer providing an income? Trans women of color are arrested all the time for drug use and possession, and usually shipped off to a men's prison. No one knows what to do with transgender inmates. There are so many trans women who can't afford surgery that end up in men's prisons even though they have breasts and don't look like men, and so many more who end up in solitary confinement the entire time because no one knows what to do with them. It's a huge problem, and we need to decrease the number of reasons that trans women are getting sent off to prison in the first place. Decriminalizing petty drug use is one of the ways to do that.

RAFAEL

I work for a social-justice organization, and one of our major projects focuses on inmate rights advocacy. Look at any prison in the U.S., and you're going to see a lot of poor, uneducated people of color. In America you have the right to a fair trial, but that doesn't mean you're going to get one. If you can't afford a good lawyer, good luck to your trial being very just.

There have been some recent high-profile cases of trans women of color being jailed in men's prisons like CeCe McDonald.[4] The media attention around her case has been good for us because people are realizing what a big issue the prison industrial complex is in the lives of trans folk. Our organization works with transgender and intersex individuals who are imprisoned in jails, prisons, holding cells, and immigration detention centers. We try to provide them with support services, and we work with a group of lawyers who offer pro-bono legal representation to our clients. We've been able to advocate for inmates to have access to hormone replacement therapy, electrolysis, and competent trans health care. We've also been able to get a few inmates moved to different facilities that better accommodate their gender identities.

NATALIE

Law enforcement officials have certain rules about how we deal with different people when we arrest them. If we need to do a pat down or a strip search on a man, we're supposed to have a male officer do it. If the person is female, we need a female officer. It protects the person being searched and protects the officer from sexual-harassment accusations. But what happens when the person we're dealing with is transgender? I've encountered trans men who pass very well as male but who haven't had bottom surgery and don't want a male officer patting them down yet say nothing because they

---

4. CeCe McDonald is a trans woman of color who was sentenced to forty-one months in a men's prison in 2012 for the death of a man who attacked her. She was released in January 2014, after serving nineteen months in prison.

are too concerned about what the officer's reaction will be if they tell him that they need a female officer.

In any profession there are bad seeds. It's a reality. I know far too many trans people who haven't been able to change the gender marker on their ID. They are all terrified of being pulled over on a dark stretch of highway because they don't know if they will come out of the situation unscathed. There are officers who use excessive force, and there are officers who definitely abuse their positions of power. However, there are a lot of officers who joined the force because they wanted to make a difference and who want to uphold justice. These are the ones who truly want to protect and serve.

I may not ever be able to reach the rogues, but most officers want to learn how they can help others and do their jobs better. That's why I started training squadrons on how to work with transgender suspects and inmates. It started with my own station first. My boss asked me to lead some diversity trainings that focused on LGBT issues. To my surprise, everyone was extremely attentive and asked very informed questions. A few weeks later, my chief told me that he wanted me to go to the state trooper office and give the same trainings. From there it snowballed: I give two to four trainings at different stations each month. I occasionally feel tokenized, but I can put those feelings aside because I know that the work that I'm doing is invaluable.

WENDY

I worked for a multinational corporation as an investment broker. I came out at work and told my boss discreetly that I was planning to transition. He told me that it wouldn't be a problem and directed me to human resources. He did and said all of the correct things to my face, so I thought I was in the clear.

A few days after, I overheard a few of my coworkers talking about me. They whispered about my plans to transition. Of course, I knew where they heard the information: I had only told one person. I didn't want to confront my boss, so I let it go at first. Unfortunately, news that juicy spread like wildfire, and I was soon working in a truly inhospitable environment. People left hate notes on my desk, keyed my car in the parking lot, and threw away my lunch. It was like being in junior high and having to deal with bullies on a daily basis. For Christ's sake, I'm an adult! I shouldn't have to deal with this.

Every time I was met with hostility I filed a detailed complaint. Within a few months of coming out, I was fired. The formal reason I was given was that I wasn't a "team player." I had filed too many complaints about my coworkers harassing me, so I was seen as being unwilling to work with others. I knew this was a load of hooey, so I sued for wrongful termination and won. I'm sure that my ex-boss would be extremely upset to know that I used the money I was awarded to pay for my surgeries. [laughs]

I think it is really important for trans folk not to let themselves be bullied and badgered. I have met a number of other people who have been fired or quit because their work environment became too hostile while they were transitioning. I sued because employers need to learn that they can't treat people like that. They need to learn not to mess with us trans folk. We're not just going to take it lying down. Not everyone has the resources or education to handle a lawsuit, but those of us who do have a certain obligation to use our resources for change. We have to fight because no one else is going to do it for us. I knew that taking legal action would set some precedents at the corporation I had worked for. In fact, they have a slew of new policies on how to accommodate diverse gender identities in the work place, and it's a direct result of them losing the lawsuit.

WILSON

I really want to be a lawyer when I grow up. Lots of trans people need lawyers, and we still need to get laws for marriage equality and adoption and all sorts of things. In some states you can't even change your name or gender on your birth certificate or driver's license. That's crazy! We need more lawyers who want to fight for LGBT causes, so that's what I'm going to do.

Activism doesn't have to be overtly political; it can also be as simple as taking the time to celebrate marginalized identities.

MOSLEY

Queer BOIS is the brainchild of one of my best friends, who is based out of Atlanta. A lot of our conversations over the years have focused on the fact that we don't see masculine of center identities reflected in many spaces, queer or otherwise, in terms of how that identity affects different facets of our lives. We would talk for hours, and one of the topics we would come back to a lot was business etiquette. When you talk about interviews, you hear that ladies wear this, and men wear that. I'm not in a space where either men's attire or women's attire really fits my identity, so how should I dress in the business world? Gender identity and expression become very salient for those of us who are nonbinary, simply because of the ways we present ourselves physically and the clothes we adorn ourselves with.

My friend and I were constantly butting up against these conversations, so we said, "Why don't we start a website that can serve as a place for people from all over the world to share ideas and exhibit different elements of style and expression? We can bring together people who are having the same concerns as we are, while celebrating their identities."

BOIS is an acronym for Business, Opulence, Investment, and Style, which are often things that people would never even consider being part of a queer person's identity. Queer people are often not thought of in business terms or as being professionals, academics, or people who contribute to society in tangible ways. Opulence shows itself through our love to splurge on the same things you see in GQ or Esquire. Investment means investing in ourselves, in our communities, and in education. Investment is really important because we often don't get included in spaces of professional and personal development. Style is a broad understanding of not only personal branding but also maintaining knowledge of who you are and how you choose to express yourself. Queer BOIS is a space to talk across all of these elements with a masculine-of-center lens.

A big portion of the project is awareness. It's very difficult to engage with anything if you're not even aware that it's there. A lot of the feedback that we get from people outside of the queer community, and even some within, is, "Oh wow, I didn't even realize that this was a thing. I didn't realize that there were QPOC [queer people of color] who dress in a way that blurs gender lines, or that there were ways you could dress to embody a certain persona."

The site has an everyday element to it. We want to talk about the issues with finding a culturally competent mental-health or physical-health practitioner or provider. We also want to talk about how to tie a bowtie. We try to make sure that we're talking holistically about these intersections. We do sort of slant the site toward women of color; however, we have women and trans men from all different kinds of backgrounds.

BLAKE

Representation is incredibly important, but members of minority groups often cannot easily point to examples of positive role models or strong representatives. As an older person in the community, I feel that it is my duty to mentor youth and help guide the way for those who are taking the reins behind me. When my generation dies, the movement will fall into their hands, and we must teach them how to be strong leaders. I teach disability studies during the school year, and while I'm at the university I mentor many of the transgender and Native students. If I can serve as a role model to them, it's important that I do so. During the summers, I go home to mentor and tutor youth on the Fort Mojave Reservation. It's good for these young kids to see that they can leave the rez and make something of themselves, and it's even better for them to see how important it is to return to the rez and give back to the community.

FELIPE

For an engineering company, the one I work for is pretty progressive. They were one of the first engineering companies to be listed in HRC's [Human Rights Campaign] Corporate Equality Index. We have a very strong office of Diversity and Inclusion. Within the office, there are subgroups that focus on race, age, and LGBT issues. We have a very robust intranet at my job, and I added myself anonymously to the LGBT e-mail listserv. There are only two administrators who know that I belong to that group, and they're very good about keeping quiet. I know that they have my back.

The LGBT issues group has a monthly tele-meeting where you can call in. You can talk if you want to, or you can just listen and not even introduce yourself. They announced at one of those meetings that they were willing to send a few people to the Out and Equal Conference in Washington, D.C. I indicated that I was interested and wrote up a proposal. One other person and I were selected to attend, and it was a really awesome experience. I love that my company was willing to send me. The other guy worked out of our Atlanta office so there was no issue of him outing me at work. After the conference, I had to complete a write-up, but I didn't have to do a presentation because I listed on my application that I was stealth.

It's really difficult to be completely stealth and to still find ways to engage in activism. My company has allowed me to maintain my safety and my stealth status locally, while representing my company at a national LGBT conference. Had I worked in any other office, I may have been able to do more than just a write-up coming out of the conference, but as it is, I have to remain stealth. There aren't too many open-minded people where I work, and if there are, they are as sneaky as me about it.

Identification Is Action

There are many ways to engage in activism. Although protests and large events often get the most recognition, it is equally important to highlight instances of everyday activism.

TAYLOR

Loud, raucous protests aren't exactly my style. I prefer to take a more academic approach. A lot of the progress that we see in the LGBT community has come from academic thinking and research about gender and sexuality. It starts in the ivory tower and disseminates from there. My degrees are in genetics and anthropology, and if I'm going to contribute to the advancement of the community, it will probably be through research.

SETH

I still consider myself a community activist and organizer. I speak at a whole bunch of conferences, and I'm publishing a paper of research that I've done on the effects of testosterone on trans men in terms of mental health. I'm involved in research, support counseling, educational outreach, and advocacy. I still do all that stuff, but I'm no longer organizing large events on the scale that I was before.

OLIVIA

Christianity has not always been a welcoming space for LGBT people. In many churches, this is still the case. I don't go out on the streets to preach love and acceptance, but I make sure that I use my pulpit to show how welcoming the light of God can be to everyone. People cite various biblical verses to prove that homosexuality is a sin, or that being transgender is a sin. When I minister about those verses, I try to put them in a historical and cultural context so that people think about the meaning of the words in a new way.

Other times, I focus on verses that I find really inspiring and that I feel show us that God loves us regardless of sexual orientation or gender expression. When people tell me that Leviticus says that lying with another man is an abomination, I like to counter it with Romans 14:13–14. The passage states, "Let us therefore no longer pass judgment on one another, but resolve instead never to put a stumbling block or hindrance in the way of another. I know and am persuaded in the Lord Jesus that nothing is unclean in itself; but it is unclean for anyone who think it unclean."

I may not be able to convince everyone that God loves and accepts homosexuals and transexuals, but I can usually help them realize that it is not their place to pass judgment on their neighbors, and that's a good place to start.

RUSS

I'm really into Deaf poetry. People always raise an eyebrow when I say that, but it's an actual art form, and it's really cool. Poetry in American Sign Language [ASL] isn't about rhyming, of course. It's more about making your hands transition from one sign to another in a really fluid and beautiful motion. Usually in ASL, you have a dominant hand and the other hand is basically a base. In poetry, you forget normal conventions like that. There's a famous Deaf poet named Patrick Graybill who has a poem called "Reflections." Throughout the poem, his left and right hand reflect one another, which is something that would never happen in regular conversation. Sign-language poetry is about creating beautiful ways to express yourself. Most of the time you don't have to have much knowledge of ASL to appreciate and understand the majority of it.

I got into Deaf poetry while I was at Gallaudet. It's a really popular activity there, and it has historically been used as a method of protest and dissention. As a trans person, poetry is my activism. I make a lot of videos and upload them to the Internet, and I perform in Deaf spaces wherever I can. My poetry is really about how my queer identity and my identity as a Deaf person intersect. Suffice it to say that as a trans, Deaf, queer person, my dating pool is really small. [laughs] It's really frustrating to try and navigate dating, so a lot of my poetry is about relationships and identity politics. People tend to be more touched by personal narrative than they are by facts and figures, so I tell poetic stories about my relationship failures and about navigating the world as a trans person.

MIRIAM

I started a group at my Hillel for LGBTQ Jews. There are a lot of us, and I wanted to be able to connect with other people who have the same faith and ethnic background that I do. We get together and cook and share various blessings that we've come across. A friend of mine wrote an alternative *birkat erusin* [blessing of betrothal] for same-sex weddings, and another one of our members has a blessing that he recites each time he binds his chest.

MOSLEY

Creating Queer BOIS was a labor of love, but it was and is healing for us too. It's a way to connect with others who are like us and to say, "We're out here, and you're not alone."

Queer BOIS is also about activism. We are at this point where it can be an educative tool for some people to build awareness, but there are also people who use the site for style tips or for health and wellness tips. People come to the site in a different place, and I think that's the beauty of it. Many of our contributors do identify as activists in a variety of roles. Sometimes people have this really one-dimensional idea of what activism is. Talking is action. Identification is action. Having representation and fighting for representation regardless of how you do that—that is action; that is activism. In black feminist thought we talk about how the personal is political. So the fact that people are living as masculine of center and the fact that we're celebrating this means that the site is a form of activism.

ASH

I identify most consistently somewhere along the lines of farm-boy. I'm really just not satisfied with the more common identity descriptors that are used in the Portland, Oregon, queer population. A lot of the queer folk here tend to be really snotty, and if you don't wear enough glitter or have the correct asymmetrical haircut, you're not queer enough to fit in. I'm not really a tomboy because I'm not really into trucks or motorcycles. I'm usually covered in dirt wearing Carhartts. When I think of myself, gender is not the primary identifier I would use. I view myself most strongly in terms of occupation, but when I add gender, my identity goes from farmer to farmboy. Hormones aren't part of my narrative, and I'm perfectly fine with that.

JAIME

I identify as a somewhat transmasculine genderqueer person, and I use singular "they" for a pronoun. "He" doesn't feel right; "she" doesn't feel right. I'm fairly androgynous, so when people don't know what to call me, they will usually default to *they*. This is technically grammatically incorrect in English, but people do it all the time because we don't have any standard gender-neutral pronouns for humans. Using gender-neutral pronouns also makes people think a lot harder about what they are saying and the assumptions that they are making.

DAKOTA

I don't really care about pronouns, and I let people use whatever is most comfortable for them. When I'm in a really queer space, I'll use *ze* and *hir*. These pronouns sound awkward in speech and look awkward when you write them. It's a very political statement to use gender-neutral pronouns, because it not only rocks the binary gender paradigm [but] also gets people to ask questions and helps to start the education process.

CAMERON

I use *transexual* probably more often than *transgender*. Within that, I sort of identify as a little more femmy and faggy as well, and as a gay man within that.

I think I use transexual because it sparks a lot of conversations with people within the trans community. Especially in the youth movement that I work in, a lot of people don't like the word transexual in terms of kids, because they think it's over sexualizing. And they think anything to do with sex shouldn't be associated with kids under the age of eighteen. But I like it because sex is a big part of positive self-identity for me. It does have drawbacks because when you're a trans person, people automatically think that your body is for public consumption and they can ask questions about it, and those who are curious about sex see you as a kind of avenue for their curiosity. I like towing that middle ground.

I like the term transgender, but it just feels a little broader to me because it can encompass everybody from genderqueer to whatever. I think it's silly when people don't use the word transexual for kids because this particular generation has spent so much time thinking about language in terms of pronouns that proscribing what language they can use before they even get their hands on it seems idiotic. They can obviously take care of it themselves.

There's Always Going to Be a Son of a Bitch Who Doesn't Like Peach Cobbler

SETH

In 2004, an anonymous e-mail went out to a bunch of listservs in the Bay Area. It was truly anonymous; to this day no one has taken credit for writing it. It said, "Let's all meet and dress up and be fabulous for a trans march." Previously, we used to go to the Dyke March every year, wearing red armbands to support trans inclusion. The e-mail said, "Feel free to add, embellish and contribute in any way to make this event fabulous."

I had just organized a Tranny Picnic in Dolores Park, the same place where the march was going to be held, a month prior. I thought I could get some of the same performers to come back. I contacted performers and politically connected trans folks and got someone to volunteer to bring DJ equipment to the park. We spread the announcement everywhere, primarily through e-mail listservs.

We had our first Trans March in June of 2004, and there were about two thousand people who showed up.

Normally, to organize an event of that scale, you have to go through channels to get the proper permits or you can face legal repercussions. The primary reason we didn't get arrested was because Critical Mass, a bike group that sort of takes over the streets in San Francisco, happened to arrive at the moment our march started and they cleared the street for us. It was beautiful timing. There was a small organization of people who held onto an altar they had made for Trans Day of Remembrance that they brought to the end of the march.

The march became something that I took on organizing for the next five years. I got funding from Good Vibes, which at the time was a co-op, not a company. That was really important to me because I didn't want any corporate funding. I didn't want a Bud Light sponsorship. It was important to me to keep it DIY and community based. The next year I had just enough funding to get a flatbed truck to use as a stage. I had a whole line of performers. Theresa Sparks was the police commissioner (and she's a trans woman), and she made sure police didn't bug us for blocking the streets that second year. That was also really important to me, considering the state of the jail and prison system, that trans folks not get arrested. I had ASL interpreters from the very beginning. I tried my absolute best to make sure that the stage performers represented as much diversity as I could reach out to in regard to age, gender, ethnicity, and ability.

The third year, I got a small committee of people together. I was able to get a little more funding from a grant. I was able to get a stage together, which we shared with the Dyke March. I could get full performing groups on stage. We had troupes of drag performers, a sound guy, and full bands. We started getting a lot of media attention, and I was on TV a few times speaking about the mission of the march, which was, in my view, equality, basic rights, and stopping discrimination against trans folks. It was still an all-volunteer event. I wasn't able to pay people, but we had just enough money to fly in Leslie Feinberg.[5] I wanted to pay performers overall, but it wasn't possible with the funding that we had.

The event kept getting bigger in the fourth and fifth years. I was able to get a five-thousand-dollar-per-year grant from the city of San Francisco to maintain the march by working with several assembly people and the senator. Senator Mark Leno had just passed a bill to add gender identity/expression to the list of things you can't discriminate against in the state of California. Former senator Carole Migden had just passed a law making it so that teachers in public schools had to stop kids who were using homophobic hate speech. The legal protections were ramping up, and Mark and Carole wanted to be recognized in our community as allies, so I had them up on stage speaking to the community. I had a lineup of performers that started at three in the afternoon and went until seven. In the fourth and fifth years, when the march was really popular, the performers started arguing with me because they all wanted the prime-time slot. I realized I didn't know how to deal with their competitiveness: I was overwhelmed.

By 2009, the activities I was running were financially solid. There was a bunch of people who wanted to get involved with the march. They were starting to say that I was too radical, or too much of an anarchist. There were also some people who were saying that we didn't have enough trans women of color in the organizing committee—that was definitely true. There were people who wanted to do more outreach to that community, and they had more access than I did. It was a good time for me to step down and pursue other projects. I had been organizing Gender Pirates, the support groups, and the speakers' bureaus for going on nine years in total. I had graduated from my MSW [master's of social work] program, and I needed to get a job. I stepped down from the majority of those groups,

5. Prominent author of trans literature and figure in the trans-rights movement. Ze helped bring the word *transgender* to prominence in its use as an umbrella term in hir work *Transgender Warriors*. Ze also served as one of the organizers of Camp Trans.

and I got a full-time job doing crisis social work for the county of Alameda.

MOSLEY

Getting flak is part of activism, and that has been true for Queer BOIS. For some folks we're not urban enough, for some people we're not black enough, for some people we're not trans inclusive enough, [and] for some folks we don't do enough talking about more things around identity and oppression, we're not political enough, or we're too political. When people send us scathing criticisms, I always think, "(a) Do you not realize how much time and energy it takes to do this? and (b) Thank you for being engaged enough to send us this, because if you didn't care about it we wouldn't even be having these conversations right now."

Critique at least lets us know that these dialogues are happening. We take it in stride. It's really important to recognize that we're evolving. The site has taken on it's own kind of identity based on feedback that we've gotten as we move forward. We're constantly sorting through that feedback, affirming some of it, and discarding some of it, but making sure we're staying true to who we are. I think there is beauty in the fact that these arguments and conversations are happening. We try to be as authentic to our goal and our core as we can. It's like fishing: you're putting it out there with the hope that someone will bite it.

There's a Dolly Parton quote that's goes something along the lines of, "You could be the sweetest, most delicious Georgia peach, but there's always going to be a son of a bitch who doesn't like peach cobbler."

HUGO

I've been a support system, I've been an advocate, and I'm just tired. I don't want to have to keep doing it. I don't want to answer the same questions over and over and over again. I've been doing this for ten years, and I don't want to have to teach the next generation.

Activism rotates. You do your bit, you help as long as you can, and then you've got to take care of yourself. People younger in transition want their activism and their experience, and we need to let them take the reins.

CATHERINE

I look around at these young trans kids who pass beautifully because they got to take hormone blockers when they were still prepubescent and transition to hormones as teens. Many of them will never need the surgeries I had to have in order to pass. They will never face the same violence and ridicule as the people in my generation did. When I look around and see these kids transitioning, and these kids who have family support, I know that every battle we waged was worth it.

GLOSSARY OF GENERAL TERMS

What follows is a very basic listing of terminology and their definitions, which were used in this work. It is not comprehensive. The definitions are contestable, ever changing, and might not speak to the experiences or identities of many.

ace / See asexuality.

agender / An identity that describes a feeling or state of being genderless. Agender people tend to feel that their gender lies somewhere in between masculine and feminine, or beyond a masculine/feminine spectrum of gender.

aggressive / Typically describes masculine-presenting lesbian women. This term is used predominantly in black, or African American, communities.

androgynous / Often describes someone whose gender cannot be clearly discerned.

asexuality / Often described as the absence of sexuality. Asexual (or ace) individuals often do not experience sexual attraction to others, though they often have affectional feelings toward others.

assigned female at birth (AFAB) / A female gender proscribed or assigned to a person when they were born, usually based on their external genitalia. Sometimes also FAAB.

assigned gender / The gender proscribed or assigned to a person when they are born, usually based on their external genitalia.

assigned male at birth (AMAB) / A male gender proscribed or assigned to a person when they were born, usually based on their external genitalia. Sometimes also MAAB.

bear / Often a large, muscular, or chubby gay or bisexual man or trans man with copious body or facial hair.

binding / Flattening one's chest to make the appearance of a male chest. Often done with ace bandages or compression shirts known as binders.

bisexual / A person emotionally, romantically, or sexually attracted to both males or men and females or women. Attraction is not necessarily evenly split between sexes and genders.

boi / Usually a masculine woman, genderqueer individual, or young trans man.

bottom / (1) A noun describing a sexual position, especially in LGB sexual relationships. Often means the recipient of the sexual activity. (2) A verb describing the act of fulfilling said sexual position. Sometimes called catcher.

bottom surgery / A term for genital-reassignment surgery used primarily in transmasculine communities.

butch / Often a lesbian with a masculine gender expression. However, this identity is sometimes claimed by gay or bisexual men as well.

cisgender / A person whose gender identity and expression conforms to the gender they were assigned at birth.

cissexual / A person whose gender identity conforms to their biological sex.

coming out / Can refer to one's acceptance of one's own sexual orientation or gender identity, or to sharing one's sexual orientation or gender identity with others. Traditionally used to describe sexual orientation as opposed to gender identity.

cosplay / Short for costume play. A type of performance art where people role-play a character while wearing costumes in any venue apart from theater. It's often associated with gaming, geek, and nerd culture.

cross-dresser / A person who wears the clothing associated with a gender other than their own. Cross-dressing is typically considered a gender expression rather than a gender identity.

crossplay / A subcategory of cosplay wherein the character being portrayed is a different sex than the person playing the character, or the character itself is being portrayed as a different sex (e.g., a female Superman or a male Catwoman).

disclosure / Can refer to one's acceptance of one's own gender identity or sexual orientation, or to sharing one's gender identity or sexual orientation with others. Traditionally used to describe gender identity as opposed to sexual orientation.

disorders of sexual development / Any number of conditions affecting the hormonal, chromosomal, anatomical, or reproductive system of a person, causing them to fall outside of the typical definitions of male or female. Previously, disorders of sexual development were called intersex conditions or hermaphroditic conditions.

dyke / A pejorative slur that is sometimes reclaimed as a positive identity label. Usually used by lesbians or masculine women.

estrogen / Hormone used by some transfeminine individuals to achieve desired secondary-sex characteristics. Must often be paired with additional antiandrogens or progestins.

fae / From fairy or faerie, usually used to identify an effeminate man or trans man. Fae (or "fay") is typically a gender identity/expression rather than a sexuality.

faggot / A pejorative slur that is sometimes reclaimed as a positive identity label. Usually used by gay or effeminate men.

female-assigned at birth (FAAB) / A female gender proscribed or assigned to a person when they were born, usually based on their external genitalia. Sometimes also AFAB.

female to male (FTM, F to M, F2M) / This phrasing emphasizes both assigned and chosen gender and represents a person who was assigned female at birth but who now identifies or expresses their gender as masculine. Many FTMs transition socially, physically, or psychologically.

femme / Often a lesbian with an effeminate gender expression. However, this identity is sometimes claimed by gay or bisexual men as well.

gay / A man emotionally, romantically, or sexually attracted to males or men.

gender / Refers to the socially constructed roles, activities, behaviors, and attributes that a given society assigns to groups based on their sex.

gender-confirmation surgeries / A recent umbrella term that encompasses all surgical procedures intended to affirm one's desired gender.

gender dysphoria / (1) The official diagnosis that trans folk have to obtain from a mental-health practitioner in order to access hormones or surgeries through the Standards of Care. Gender identity disorder appeared in the *Diagnostic and Statistical Manual of Mental Disorders* (DSM-IV) in 1980. The name was changed to gender dysphoria in the DSM-V. (2) State of hyperawareness and discomfort of one's gender or sex. Often when a person's gender expression or physical body does not match their gender identity, they will experience gender dysphoria.

gender expression / How one conveys one's gender identity outwardly to others.

gender identity / A person's internal sense of belonging to a particular gender category.

gender identity disorder / The official diagnosis that every trans person has to obtain from a mental-health practitioner in order to access hormones or surgeries through the Standards of Care. First appeared in the *Diagnostic and Statistical Manual of Mental Disorders* (DSM-IV) in 1980. The name was changed to gender dysphoria in the DSM-V.

gender-neutral pronouns / Sets of pronouns that deviate from he/him/his and she/her/hers. See yo/yos and ze/hir/hirs for usage examples.

genderqueer/gender nonconforming/gender fluid / (1) Terms that often designate a nonnormative or nonbinary gender identity or expression. (2) Can refer to someone who is not comfortable identifying as a man or woman. (3) Can refer to a gender identity that purposefully breaks social norms or rules regarding gender. (4) A term that falls under the transgender umbrella. The person might or might not wish to take social, medical, or surgical steps to physically or socially bring their body or gender expression in line with the gender with which they identify.

genital-reassignment (or reconstruction) surgery (GRS) / A surgical process wherein a person's genitals are reconstructed to more closely align with the sex with which they identify. This often consists of vaginoplasty for male-to-female individuals and metoidioplasty, scrotoplasty, or phalloplasty for female-to-male individuals. Once called sexual-reassignment surgery (SRS), it is now frequently categorized as gender-confirmation surgery.

heteronormativity / The presumption that being heterosexual is the norm.

heterosexual / A person emotionally, romantically, or sexually attracted to people of a different sex or gender from their own. Also called straight.

homosexual / A person emotionally, romantically, or sexually attracted to people of the same sex or gender as their own. Also called gay or lesbian.

hormone replacement therapy (HRT) / A medical process wherein a person takes cross-sex hormones to achieve secondary-sex characteristics, which appear as masculinization or feminization of the body. Can also include puberty-suppressing medications for youth.

intersex / A person born with any number of conditions affecting their hormonal, chromosomal, anatomical, or reproductive systems causing them to fall outside of the typical definitions of male or female. Intersex conditions are now called disorders of sexual development.

lesbian / A woman emotionally, romantically, or sexually attracted to females or women.

lesbian, gay, bisexual, and transgender (LGBT) / Often written LGBTQI to include queer and intersex communities. Frequently includes many additional letters and is often used as an umbrella term for queer communities.

male-assigned at birth (MAAB) / A male gender proscribed or assigned to a person when they were born, usually based on their external genitalia. Sometimes also AMAB.

male to female (MTF, M to F, M2F) / This phrasing emphasizes both assigned and chosen gender. A person who was assigned male at birth but who now identifies or expresses their gender as feminine. Many MTFs transition socially, physically, or psychologically.

masculine of center (MOC) / A term for masculine women used primarily in communities of color.

pass / (verb) To be successfully recognized by others (usually strangers) as one's desired gender. This term is viewed as problematic by many as it implies a negative binary wherein gender is an act that can be failed. For further discussion of gender performativity and passing see Mattilda Bernstein Sycamore's *Nobody Passes* and Judith Halberstam's *Female Masculinity*.

polyamory / Usually refers to having emotional, romantic, or sexual relationships with more than one partner.

queer / (1) A formerly pejorative slur that has been reclaimed as a positive identity label. Often queer is used in a strongly political or radical manner to designate going against mainstream expectations in regards to gender, sexuality, or politics. (2) An umbrella term that replaces LGBT and other similar acronyms. (3) A term that usually designates a nonnormative sexual orientation. (4) A term that usually designates a nonnormative gender identity or expression.

sex / Anatomical, hormonal, chromosomal, and reproductive composition of the body. Usually male, female, or intersex.

sexual-reassignment surgery / See genital-reassignment surgery.

Standards of Care / A set of guidelines for the physical and mental treatment of transgender and transexual patients. Maintained by the World Professional Association for Transgender Health.

stealth / A trans person who has transitioned, passes well as their desired gender, and chooses not to disclose their trans status to others.

straight / See heterosexual.

stud / Typically describes masculine-presenting lesbian women. This term is used predominantly in black or African American communities.

testosterone / Hormone used by some transmasculine individuals to achieve desired secondary-sex characteristics. Often simply called "T."

top / (1) A noun describing a sexual position, especially in LGB sexual relationships. Often means the provider of the sexual activity. (2) A verb describing the act of fulfilling said sexual position. Sometimes called pitcher.

top surgery / Surgical procedures involving the chest or breasts. Usually includes a mastectomy for female-to-male patients and breast augmentation for male-to-female patients. Can also be called chest-reconstruction surgery.

tranny / A pejorative slur that is sometimes reclaimed as a positive identity label. Usually used by trans women. There is contention regarding whether or not trans men should be allowed to reclaim this word.

transensual / Often a person emotionally, romantically, or sexually attracted to transgender or gender nonconforming individuals.

transexual / Often a transgender individual who has transitioned surgically or has an intent to transition surgically or medically. Although spelled with two *s*'s by the medical community, it is sometimes spelled with one *s* when used as an identity label. This is often viewed as an outdated term by younger trans individuals.

transfeminine / The adjective form of trans woman.

transgender (trans) / (1) An umbrella term used to describe many different people whose gender identities and expressions do not conform to the gender they were assigned at birth. (2) Can describe a person who has taken social, medical, or surgical steps to physically or socially bring their body or gender expression in line with the gender with which they identify (can also be called transexual). Can also be spelled trans*, where the asterisk denotes a broad social interpretation that includes anyone who is not strictly cisgender.

transition / Often a social, medical, or surgical process wherein a person physically or socially brings their body or gender expression in line with the gender with which they identify.

trans man / A person usually assigned female at birth who has taken social, medical, or surgical steps to physically or socially masculinize his gender expression or body. This term emphasizes chosen gender as opposed to assigned gender.

transmasculine / The adjective form of trans man.

transphobia / An irrational fear or hatred of transgender or gender nonconforming people.

transvestite / A person who wears the clothing associated with a gender other than their own. Often considered an outdated term. See cross-dresser.

trans woman / A person usually assigned male at birth who has taken social, medical, or surgical steps to physically or socially feminize her gender expression or body. This term emphasizes chosen gender as opposed to assigned gender.

twink / Usually a young gay or bisexual man with very little body hair and a slender frame.

yo/yos / Gender-neutral pronouns that are most often used in communities of color. For example, "She took her dog on a walk; the dog is hers" would become "Yo took yo dog on a walk; the dog is yos."

ze/hir/hirs / Gender-neutral pronouns. For example, "She took her dog on a walk; the dog is hers" would become "Ze took hir dog on a walk; the dog is hirs."[1]

1. There are many additional gender-neutral pronouns other than yo/yos and ze/hir/hirs.

GLOSSARY OF MEDICAL TERMS

antiandrogen / Medication to reduce testosterone levels or activity in MTF
   patients. Used concurrently with estrogen to reduce the dosage of
   estrogen necessary to suppress testosterone.
binding / See glossary of general terms. Can restrict breath, cause rashes or
   cuts, increase acne, lead to rib cage deformity, and cause tissue damage.
breast augmentation / Surgical procedure to create or enhance breasts.
   Many transgender women do not elect to have breast augmentation, as
   estrogen use often induces satisfactory breast growth.
chondrolaryngoplasty / Surgical procedure to reduce the prominence of the
   Adam's apple (tracheal cartilage). Also referred to as a tracheal shave.
disorders of sexual development / See glossary of general terms.
electrolysis / Permanent removal of facial or body hair through inducing
   localized damage to the hair follicle. Most often sought by postpubertal
   MTF patients.
estrogen / Induces physical changes in MTF patients including decreased
   erectile function, decreased testicular size, breast growth, softening
   of skin, increased body fat, and cessation of male-pattern baldness.
   Other effects include decreased muscle mass, decreased libido,
   sexual dysfunction, and decreased sperm production. Side effects can
   include an increased risk for venous thromboembolic disease and
   hypertriglyceridemia.
facial feminization surgeries / A set of surgeries designed to feminize male
   facial features. Can include scalp advancement, browlift or forehead
   contouring, rhinoplasty, cheek augmentation, lip augmentation, chin
   augmentation, ramus reduction or angle of mandible reduction, skin-
   resurfacing procedures, and others.
gender dysphoria / See glossary of general terms.
gender identity disorder / See glossary of general terms.
genital-reassignment surgery / See glossary of general terms.

GnRH analogues / Used in transgender and gender-questioning youth to suppress estrogen or testosterone production, thereby delaying puberty. Often first administered when youth reach Tanner stage 2. Pubertal suppression is often followed with feminizing or masculinizing hormones.

hormone replacement therapy / See glossary of general terms.

hysterectomy / In FTM patients, the removal of the uterus. Can involve oophorectomy and salpingectomy. Might involve removal of the cervix.

intersex / See glossary of general terms.

labiaplasty / In MTF patients, the creation of labia, often from scrotal tissue. Frequently concurrent with vaginoplasty, or as a revision of vaginoplasty.

mastectomy (bilateral) / In FTM patients, the creation of a masculine chest through the removal of breasts and often the repositioning of the nipple complex.

metoidioplasty / In FTM patients, the lengthening and release of the clitoris from the hood to form a neophallus. Can include mons resection or phallus repositioning. Urethral lengthening might be performed. Scrotoplasty can occur concurrently. Vaginectomy can occur concurrently but is not always required. Also called metadoioplasty.

oophorectomy (bilateral) / In FTM patients, surgical procedure to remove the ovaries. Typically occurs concurrently with salpingectomy, or as part of radical hysterectomy.

orchiectomy (bilateral) / Removal of testicles, eliminating androgen production. Often occurs concurrently with vaginoplasty but can also precede or occur in lieu of vaginoplasty. Technique should be discussed if vaginoplasty will occur at a later time. Also known as orchidectomy or gonadectomy.

phalloplasty / In FTM patients, creation of phallus through graft tissues. Usually, involves urethral lengthening. Often includes malleable rod implant, insert, or pump to achieve erections. Can occur concurrently with scrotoplasty.

progestins / Often used concurrently with estrogen in MTF patients to promote mammary development.

salpingectomy (bilateral) / In FTM patients, surgical procedure to remove fallopian tubes. Typically occurs concurrently with oophorectomy, or as part of radical hysterectomy.

scrotoplasty / In FTM patients, surgical procedure placing implants into the labia majora to form testicles. Will often have bifid appearance if vaginectomy has not occurred.

Standards of Care / See glossary of general terms and Appendix A.

Tanner stages / Scale of physical development. For transgender children and adolescents, this scale is used to determine the appropriate onset of puberty to administer GnRH analogues.

testosterone / Induces physical changes in FTM patients including increased clitoral size, lengthening of the vocal cords, cessation of menses, breast tissue atrophy, increased growth in body and facial hair, and increased muscle mass. Other effects can include oily skin or acne, loss of hair on the scalp, and vaginal atrophy. Side effects can include an increased risk for polycythemia.

vaginectomy / In FTM patients, surgical procedure to remove all or part of the vagina. Often colpocleisis is used to remove vagina mucosa, fuse vaginal walls, and close vaginal opening. Can occur concurrently with metoidioplasty, scrotoplasty, or phalloplasty.

vaginoplasty / In MTF patients, the creation of a vagina from existing tissue, often using the technique of penile inversion. Vaginal lining might also be created from sigmoid or ascending colon. Orchiectomy can precede or occur concurrently. Labiaplasty can occur concurrently or at a later date.

APPENDIX A
Summary of Criteria for Hormone
Therapy and Surgeries

Reprinted with permission from the *Standards of Care for the Health of Transsexual, Transgender, and Gender-Nonconforming People*, 7th version (2012), by Eli Coleman, Walter Bockting, Marsha Botzer, et al., of the World Professional Association for Transgender Health (WPATH). The WPATH Standards of Care are subject to revision when new medical evidence supports relevant changes. To ensure you are referring to the latest edition of this information, please check for updates in the Publications section at www.wpath.org.

As for all previous versions of the SOC [Standards of Care], the criteria put forth in the SOC for hormone therapy and surgical treatments for gender dysphoria are clinical guidelines; individual health professionals and programs may modify them. Clinical departures from the SOC may come about because of a patient's unique anatomic, social, or psychological situation; an experienced health professional's evolving method of handling a common situation; a research protocol; lack of resources in various parts of the world; or the need for specific harm-reduction strategies. These departures should be recognized as such, explained to the patient, and documented through informed consent for quality patient care and legal protection. This documentation is also valuable to accumulate new data, which can be retrospectively examined to allow for health care—and the SOC—to evolve.

Criteria for Feminizing/Masculinizing Hormone Therapy (One Referral or Chart Documentation of Psychosocial Assessment)

1. Persistent, well-documented gender dysphoria;
2. Capacity to make a fully informed decision and to give consent for treatment;

3. Age of majority in a given country (if younger, follow the SOC for children and adolescents); [and]
4. If significant medical or mental concerns are present, they must be reasonably well controlled.

Criteria for Breast/Chest Surgery (One Referral)

Mastectomy and Creation of a Male Chest in FtM Patients:
1. Persistent, well-documented gender dysphoria;
2. Capacity to make a fully informed decision and to give consent for treatment;
3. Age of majority in a given country (if younger, follow the SOC for children and adolescents); [and]
4. If significant medical or mental health concerns are present, they must be reasonably well controlled.

Hormone therapy is not a prerequisite.

Breast Augmentation (Implants/Lipofilling) in MtF Patients:
1. Persistent, well-documented gender dysphoria;
2. Capacity to make a fully informed decision and to give consent for treatment;
3. Age of majority in a given country (if younger, follow the SOC for children and adolescents); [and]
4. If significant medical or mental health concerns are present, they must be reasonably well controlled.

Although not an explicit criterion, it is recommended that MtF patients undergo feminizing hormone therapy (minimum 12 months) prior to breast augmentation surgery. The purpose is to maximize breast growth in order to obtain better surgical (aesthetic) results.

Criteria for Genital Surgery (Two Referrals)

*Hysterectomy and Salpingo-Oophorectomy in
FtM Patients and Orchiectomy in MtF Patients:*
1. Persistent, well-documented gender dysphoria;
2. Capacity to make a fully informed decision and to give consent for treatment;
3. Age of majority in a given country;

4. If significant medical or mental health concerns are present, they must be well controlled; [and]
5. 12 continuous months of hormone therapy as appropriate to the patient's gender goals (unless hormones are not clinically indicated for the individual).

The aim of hormone therapy prior to gonadectomy is primarily to introduce a period of reversible estrogen or testosterone suppression, before a patient undergoes irreversible surgical intervention.

These criteria do not apply to patients who are having these surgical procedures for medical indications other than gender dysphoria.

Metoidioplasty or Phalloplasty in FtM Patients and Vaginoplasty in MtF Patients:

1. Persistent, well-documented gender dysphoria;
2. Capacity to make a fully informed decision and to give consent for treatment;
3. Age of majority in a given country;
4. If significant medical or mental health concerns are present, they must be well controlled;
5. 12 continuous months of hormone therapy as appropriate to the patient's gender goals (unless hormones are not clinically indicated for the individual); [and]
6. 12 continuous months of living in a gender role that is congruent with their gender identity.

Although not an explicit criterion, it is recommended that these patients also have regular visits with a mental health or other medical professional.

The criterion noted above for some types of genital surgeries—that is, that patients engage in 12 continuous months of living in a gender role that is congruent with their gender identity—is based on expert clinical consensus that this experience provides ample opportunity for patients to experience and socially adjust in their desired gender role, before undergoing irreversible surgery.

The WPATH Standards of Care are subject to revision when new medical evidence supports relevant changes. To ensure you are referring to the latest edition of this information, please check for updates in the Publications section at www.wpath.org.

APPENDIX B
Resources for Medical and
Mental Health-Care Providers

American Psychiatric Association. *Diagnostic and Statistical Manual of Mental Disorders: DSM-V.* Washington, DC: American Psychiatric Association, 2013.
Includes official criteria for diagnosing gender dysphoria in children, adolescents, and adults, as well as recommendations for medical interventions.

Bockting, Walter O., ed. *International Journal of Transgenderism.* Routledge, 1998–.
The official journal of WPATH. This peer-reviewed publication covers the social, medical, and psychological treatment of transgender individuals. Published quarterly from 1998 to the present in print and online.

Brill, Stephanie A., and Rachel Pepper. *The Transgender Child: A Handbook for Families and Professionals.* San Francisco: Cleis Press, 2008.
Provides information and resources for the families and providers of transgender and gender-nonconforming children and adolescents.

Ettner, Randi, Stan Monstrey, and A. Evan Eyler. *Principles of Transgender Medicine and Surgery.* New York: Haworth Press, 2007.
Anthology of medical, surgical, and mental-health aspects of caring for transgender patients. Discusses reproductive and fertility issues, examines best practices in providing care for juveniles and adults, and covers issues of transgender aging.

Informed Consent for Access to Trans Health (ICATH). Home page. Accessed November 24, 2014. http://www.icath.org.
An alternative model to the WPATH Standards of Care. Outlines and provides sample letters for accessing medical and surgical interventions for transgender patients using an informed-consent model.

Israel, Gianna E., and Donald E. Tarver II. *Transgender Care: Recommended Guidelines, Practical Information, and Personal Accounts.* Philadelphia: Temple University Press, 1997.

Discusses the role that physicians and mental-health-care providers should play in caring for transgender patients. This text carefully examines such topics as the role of cultural diversity, HIV/AIDS, and support systems in providing transgender care.

APPENDIX C
Recommended Reading on
Transgender Narratives and History

Bornstein, Kate, and S. Bear Bergman. *Gender Outlaws: The Next Generation*. Berkeley, CA: Seal Press, 2010.
An anthology of essays by trans and gender-nonconforming individuals who reimagine and reconceptualize the boundaries of gender.

Feinberg, Leslie. *Transgender Warriors: Making History from Joan of Arc to Dennis Rodman*. Boston: Beacon Press, 1996.
Utilizing a broad definition of "transgender," Feinberg thoroughly discusses examples of gender-transgressing characters throughout recorded history and provides new ways of thinking about gender diversity.

Girshick, Lori B. *Transgender Voices: Beyond Women and Men*. Hanover, NH: University Press of New England, 2008.
A sociological look at gender transgression. Uses narrative-based interviews to discuss the social constructs of gender, sex, and sexuality.

Meyerowitz, Joanne. *How Sex Changed: A History of Transsexuality in the United States*. Cambridge, MA: Harvard University Press, 2002.
Provides a thorough social, medical, and cultural history of transexuality in the United States. Discusses how concepts of sex and gender have changed over the past two centuries.

Stryker, Susan. *Transgender History*. Berkeley, CA: Seal Press, 2008.
Delivers detailed chronological documentation of transgender history. Covering a broad definition of transgender, this work highlights the events that helped to shape the current climate for trans folk in the United States.

INDEX

adoption, 65, 84, 182
agender identities, 72–73
agequeer identities, 24, 117
aggressives, 23n15, 83
aging, 98, 130, 132
AIDS, 159, 168–69. *See also* HIV
AIDS Coalition to Unleash Power,
    168–69
allies, 73, 89, 126, 133, 161, 162, 192;
    to people with disabilities, 126,
    133; role of, 105, 107
Americans with Disabilities Act,
    128
androgyny, 26, 74, 75, 189
asexuality, 40, 92, 117–21, 142, 159,
    160; and dysphoria, 63, 120
assimilation, 2, 8, 9, 110, 158
athleticism, 16, 65, 91
autism, 126, 132, 149, 160

backlash, 4, 175, 193
bars, 137; gay, 79, 89
bathrooms. *See* restrooms
bears, 117
Benjamin, Harry, 3, 38, 39–40
binding, 11, 55, 56, 59, 60, 145, 188
bisexuality, 19, 31, 73, 74
body contouring, 55
body image, 62, 90–95
bois, 113
bottom surgeries, 62, 64, 147, 180.

See also hysterectomy; phalloplasty;
    vaginoplasty
Bowers, Marci, 57
breasts, 12, 49, 52, 145, 179; augmen-
    tation of, 55, 74, 116; reduction of,
    56, 59. *See also* binding; mastectomy
Breedlove, Lynnee, 170
bullying, 42, 115, 132, 182
butches, 23n15, 82, 113
Butler, Judith, 5

Califia, Patrick, 5
Camp Trans, 5, 169–70, 192n5
catcalling, 11, 104, 106
Catholicism, 112
cerebral palsy, 125, 130
Christianity, 17, 111–12, 186–87
Clery Act, 161
clothing, 26, 64, 69, 94, 156, 164,
    183; gendered, 70–71, 79, 90–91.
    See also cross-dressing
coming out, 18, 23; as asexual, 118,
    160; as bisexual, 19, 31; to family,
    17, 22, 26, 30, 80; as gay, 12, 112;
    as lesbian, 18, 19, 21, 82. *See also*
    identity disclosure
communities of color, 81–82, 83, 84,
    105, 106, 113, 139–41, 163, 183–84;
    and activism, 179, 180, 188, 193;
    suspicion of, 103, 124; vocabulary
    used within, 78n1, 113, 114

transitioning without, 13, 42, 73, 77, 189; for youth, 44, 45, 109, 194. *See also* estrogen; testosterone
housing, 6; discrimination, 4, 81, 152–53; gendered, 48, 69
Human Rights Campaign, 185
hysterectomy, 55, 62, 73, 120

identification, 156; and gender markers, 17, 156–57, 165, 181, 182
identity disclosure, 2, 8, 12, 25–35, 41, 54, 80, 96; to children, 65, 84, 86; to family, 26–31, 41, 45, 72, 80–81, 95; to partners, 32–35, 55, 89–90, 115; at work, 26, 66–70, 78, 153, 161, 181–82
identity politics, 77, 100, 158, 187
incarceration, 134, 178, 179–81, 191
insurance, 44, 46, 57, 60, 107, 108, 129–30, 150, 151
Internet, 10, 24, 37, 78, 173, 175, 187; and online communities, 24, 87
intersex, 134–35, 172, 173, 180. *See also* disorders of sexual development
isolation, 23, 131, 140, 167, 168, 172

Johnson, Melissa, 56
Jorgensen, Christine, 3, 37–38, 40
Judaism, 112–13, 188; rituals of, 88, 113

kink, 62, 87, 127

labels, 13, 16n12, 22, 73, 76, 92, 104, 114
language, 2, 62, 75, 101, 113, 114, 190
Leno, Mark, 192
Lesbian Avengers, 167–68, 169–70
lesbian communities, 68, 79, 82
lesbians, 20, 45, 90, 112, 143, 158, 160, 175; and activism, 38, 168, 169–70; and coming out, 18, 19, 21, 82; and

trans identities, 39n5, 65, 114, 116, 140. *See also* aggressives; butches; studs
letter, the, 39, 40, 42–44, 46, 49–50, 56, 57, 92, 107
libido, 51, 52, 118
locker rooms, 65, 67, 91, 172. *See also* dressing rooms; restrooms

marginalization, 80, 81–82, 183; of asexual identities, 118–20; from LGB communities, 79, 80, 81, 83, 100, 153, 157–64, 190; of nonbinary identities, 74, 100, 142, 143; of people of color 81, 83, 103, 104, 107, 124; of people with disabilities, 122–24; of trans women, 5, 84, 137, 169–70. *See also* harassment
marijuana reform, 176–79
marriage, 33, 51, 139; equality, 81, 157, 174, 175–77, 182
masculine of center, 81, 90, 104, 183–84, 188
mastectomy, 36, 55, 64, 66, 73, 74, 92, 107; accessing, 56, 102–3; financing, 58, 65, 108; results, 59–60, 164
McDonald, CeCe, 180
media, 3, 38, 40, 83, 166, 180, 191; and trans representation, 14, 15, 25, 44
medroxyprogesterone, 48
menstruation, 62, 92, 143, 144, 151
Michigan Womyn's Music Festival, 5, 169–70
microaggressions, 102, 103, 122–23
Migden, Carole, 192
military, 10, 22, 33, 43, 61
misgendering, 31, 81, 147, 150, 163
mobility, 60, 122, 131, 133, 155; devices, 122, 123, 124, 125, 132
Mojave, 96, 184

monogamy, 53, 178
MTFs, 72, 169
multiple sclerosis, 123
Muñoz, José Esteban, 5
murder, 83, 136, 138, 179

name change, 17, 67, 68, 78, 150, 154,
    182
nationality, 103, 156
New Hampshire Freedom to Marry, 174
nonbinary identities, 15, 70–75,
    170, 183; disclosure of, 22, 23;
    marginalization of, 74, 100, 142,
    143

Obama, Barack, 164, 174, 175
oppression, 4, 76, 96, 97, 100, 102,
    136, 154, 193

passing, 24, 80, 90, 94–95, 109, 117,
    153, 180; as able-bodied, 121, 124,
    125; as desired gender, 13, 59,
    67–68, 117, 136, 144, 145, 154, 158;
    privilege, 80, 94, 98, 101, 136, 142,
    194; without aid, 45, 94
patriarchy, 5, 106
pediatrician, 41, 44, 130
phalloplasty, 120
pinkwashing, 109
PISSAR, 172–73
Planned Parenthood, 173
poetry, 89, 187
police, 4, 17, 30, 67, 137, 179, 191
polyamory, 68, 87, 114, 159
Portland Green Independent Commit-
    tee, 178
power dynamics, 4, 123, 179, 181
pregnancy, 128, 143
pride, 83; parades, 83, 157–58
primary care physician, 43, 44, 53, 56,
    129, 130, 148, 189

privilege, 107, 109, 163, 171; able-
    bodied, 106, 126; male, 100, 101–2,
    106
pronouns, 2, 11, 27, 31, 75, 115, 120,
    150, 160, 190; gender-neutral, 2, 65,
    75, 114, 189; preferred 36, 61, 65,
    66, 81, 141. See also misgendering
protests, 2, 5, 38, 161, 166, 167, 169,
    170, 175, 185–87
puberty, 41, 45, 52, 59; suppressing
    medications, 41, 45

Queer BOIS, 183–84, 188, 193
queer communities, 73, 74, 79, 84,
    87, 89, 176, 178; of color, 81, 161,
    183–84, 188, 193; and drug use,
    177, 178; and spaces, 68, 74, 160
queer identities, 105, 109, 161, 163,
    187; and genders, 30, 99, 104;
    and sexualities, 23, 39, 116, 118;
    umbrella of, 10, 20, 157, 164, 175;
    visibility of, 83, 158, 161, 166

racism, 81, 102, 103–4, 105, 107,
    161–62
real life experience, the, 41–42
reclamation: of language, 2, 16n12;
    of self, 91, 121
religion, 2, 7, 55, 99, 100, 110–11
reproductive justice, 173
respectability politics, 100, 153, 157–60
restrooms, 70, 98, 142, 165; and
    accessibility, 128–29, 172–73;
    public, 79, 98, 137, 172. See also
    locker rooms; dressing rooms
role models, 44, 84, 169, 184

safer-sex, 119, 142–43, 169
Safe2Pee, 173
same-gender loving, 78
Sedgwick, Eve Kosofsky, 5